The Sacramental Sea

The Sacramental Sea

A Spiritual Voyage through Christian History

Edmund Newell

To Ella

with very best wishes,

Ed

DARTON · LONGMAN + TODD

First published in Great Britain in 2019 by
Darton, Longman and Todd Ltd
1 Spencer Court
140–142 Wandsworth High Street
London SW18 4JJ

ISBN 978-0-232-53396-5

A catalogue record for this book is available from the British Library

Phototypeset by Kerrypress Ltd, St Albans, Hertfordshire, AL3 8JL
Printed and bound in Great Britain by Short Run Press, Exeter

For Susan, Sarah and Matthew

Contents

Preface

The idea of writing this book came, appropriately, from out of the blue. In the spring of 2007 I was invited to lead the BBC Radio 4 *Easter Sunrise Service*. At the time I was a Canon of St Paul's Cathedral, and I was asked by the producer to offer an early morning reflection for Easter Day while looking across London from the Golden Gallery at the top of the cathedral's famous dome. This proved more problematic than expected, for although the view is undoubtedly magnificent it is not the sort that naturally stirs religious feelings – at least in me. Gazing across an immense urban landscape speaks to me more of human ingenuity than of God. So I had to work hard to develop a reflection that was uplifting for listeners and yet honest to my own thoughts and feelings. It proved to be an interesting and important spiritual exercise, and the catalyst for writing this book.

In preparing for the broadcast I became aware of the importance of the natural world – especially the sea – to me spiritually. Looking down from the dome I could see the river Thames; the early morning sunlight shimmering on its surface, snaking through the city. The presence of water in the urban landscape brought a quality to the vista that is hard to put into words. It reminded me that the view which stirs my soul perhaps more than any other is to look out across the Bristol Channel from one of Exmoor's magnificent hog's back cliffs. Had I been asked to broadcast a reflection from, say, Foreland Point, one of the highest cliffs in the country, near Lynton and Lynmouth where I grew up and to where I return time and time again, writing the script for the broadcast would have been relatively straightforward, as there is so much I could have said about the view out to sea.

The experience of recording that service turned my attention to the question it raised: why does the sea and coastline have such an impact on me? Is it because of its familiarity or association with my childhood? After all, when I was less than one year old my family moved to the North Devon coast. From our house, perched on a hillside some 600 feet above sea level, we looked across the Bristol Channel. I remember as a child watching ships go by and wondering where they had come from and where they were going. I remember, too, the excitement of watching the hull of Brunel's *Great Britain* being towed to Bristol from the Falkland Islands, and the unexpected sight of a submarine surfacing as I was looking out to sea. At night, I was often transfixed by the beams cast by the lighthouse on Foreland Point and the distant lights of South Wales, wondering what it was like to be on the coast across the channel, which seemed another world to me. From my bedroom I could also hear the roar of the waterfalls from the nearby West Lyn river as it plunged down towards the sea, and where, in August 1952, its waters converged with those of the East Lyn to wreak havoc by ripping out the heart of the seaside village of Lynmouth and its community, by taking 34 lives. Later, I became a regular visitor to Lundy, the island twelves miles off the North Devon coast that I could see from my school in Ilfracombe. On Lundy I became mesmerised by watching sunlight shimmer on the vast expanse of Atlantic Ocean stretching out to the to the west, and it is where I had the eerie experience of climbing down a cliff to explore the wreck of the *Kaaksburg*, a German cargo ship that had run aground on the island in the winter of 1980, fortunately without loss of life.

The sense of being at home by the sea is clearly important to me, but numerous conversations spanning my work on this book have made it abundantly clear that the call of the sea, in its various forms, is widespread and can be deeply spiritual. Whether it is living by the sea, sailing, swimming, surfing, exploring beaches and rock-pools, or walking along sea-cliffs, many of those who have shared their experiences with me have spoken about an attraction to the sea in almost religious terms. I began to wonder why.

What I was also aware of, but had not thought about systematically before embarking on this project, is how frequently the sea is mentioned in the Bible, often with negative connotations. This led me to consider two further questions: do the stories of Noah and the Flood, Jonah and the whale, the parting of the Red Sea, Paul being shipwrecked, and the many other biblical references to the sea share anything in common; and why do so many of these stories portray the sea negatively? These, then, were my starting points, and the book flowed out of these initial questions.

⌒

Given that the idea for this book originated at St Paul's Cathedral, which I left in 2008, it is appropriate that the impetus to finish it came in 2017 when I was invited back to take part in the Just Water programme – an international environmental project organised by St Paul's in collaboration with St Paul's Cathedral Melbourne, St George's Cathedral Cape Town, and Trinity Church Wall Street. As well as returning to speak, I contributed an earlier version of this work to a special edition of the *Anglican Theological Review* linked to the Just Water project, under the title 'The Sacramental Sea' (volume 100, no. 1, Winter 2018), and it used here by permission of the *Anglican Theological Review*. Writing this article honed my thinking on how to structure the book, thanks to the challenging and incisive comments of the editors of the special edition of the *Review*, Scott Bayder and Barbara Ridpath, then Director of St Paul's Institute.

I am grateful to many others as well who, in various ways, have helped me along the way. My former colleagues at St Paul's provided me with the time and space to begin the research during a sabbatical. Much of the sabbatical was spent at the Department of Religious Studies at the University of Wales, Lampeter (now University of Wales, Trinity St David). My time at Lampeter proved immensely productive and enjoyable, and I learned much from discussions with members of the department, especially Thomas O'Loughlin and Jonathan Wooding. Participants at the fourth Blue Mind Summit in Cornwall, theology summer schools at Oxford and Lampeter universities, a retreat at Lee Abbey, a quiet day at Douai Abbey, and a seminar at Westminster Abbey Institute provided helpful comments as I tested out ideas. Sabina Alkire, Nick Bicât, Nigel Biggar, Ian Bradley, Michael Depledge, Paul Edmondson, Ishrat Hossain, Christina Li, Verena Schiller, and Brian Shoemaker have all offered suggestions, helpful comments or advice. Rosemary Peacocke and Hannah Stammers provided much needed research assistance. Zoe Bicât and Amanda Piesse read and commented on the final draft with great care and insight. Phil Hind, Kitty O'Lone, Emmy Stavropolou, and Helen Taylor have kindly helped develop related website and social media content. It has also been a pleasure to work with David Moloney, Will Parkes, and Helen Porter at Darton, Longman and Todd to bring this project to its conclusion. I am deeply grateful to them all.

There are a further six people, living and departed, without whom this book would not have been written. My parents, Ken Newell and the late Mary Newell, made the decision to take their family to live and grow up by the sea, for which I am extremely thankful. The late Robin Craig was not only an inspirational teacher of maritime history when I was an undergraduate, but a good friend who taught me how to think about the sea. Robin died a fortnight after I began working on this book, and I often wonder about the conversations we might have had if there had been opportunity to discuss the project with him. Finally, my wife, Susan, and children, Sarah and Matthew, have lived with this project – in Matthew's case, all his life – and have been my companions on numerous expeditions to coasts and islands. In the process they have endured foul weather, choppy seas and, on several occasions, violent storms when we have been camping on remote coastal sites. They have also tolerated absences from the home when I have needed time away to think and write. Without their love and support I simply would not have been able to work on this project on and off over the past eleven years, and so this book is dedicated to them.

Cumberland Lodge,
Windsor Great Park
April 2019

Introduction

Odi et amo may well be the confession of those
who consciously or blindly have surrendered their
existence to the fascination of the sea.

Joseph Conrad, *The Mirror of the Sea*

There is something about the sea that is both enticing and fearful, so much
so that, as Joseph Conrad (quoting the poet Catullus) observed, it can draw
out the strongest feeling of attraction and its conflicting shadow-side: *odi et
amo*, 'I hate and I love'. Conrad should know. In 1874, at the age of 17, Jósef
Korzeniowski, to use Conrad's real name, heard the sea's call and travelled
from his native Poland to the south of France to join the crew of the *Mont
Blanc*. As he set sail from Marseille on a voyage to Martinique so began
for Conrad a long career at sea, during which he experienced its thrill and
exhilaration, felt its peace and tranquillity, survived terrifying storms, and
watched colleagues drown. Such tragedies failed to diminish his passion for
the sea, but they certainly removed any false illusions about its attractions.
When Conrad turned to writing he became a most astute observer of life at
sea.

Conrad also wrote, 'The true peace of God begins at any spot a thousand
miles from the nearest land.'[1] The sea plays an important role in many
religions, not least Christianity, where the ambivalence Conrad describes
is particularly apparent. The majority of biblical references to the sea draw
on its negative connotations, yet there are many accounts within Christian
literature of people feeling spiritually uplifted, or close to God, on or by the
sea. This book explores these contrasting attitudes within Christianity and
shows how they have changed over time. In doing so, it seeks to show that
there is a deeply sacramental quality to the sea. 'Sacramental' can refer to
specific religious rites, such as baptism and communion. It can also refer to
something that, to quote F. W. Dillistone, 'holds more of value or significance
within it than at first meets the eye.'[2] It is this latter, broader, understanding of
'sacramental' that is used throughout this book, which seeks to show that the

sea speaks more powerfully of the complexity of our understanding of God, and our relationship with God, than perhaps anything else. As will be seen, this adds a particular theological dimension to the pressing environmental issues of marine pollution and rising sea levels.

A key reason for the sea's sacramental quality is that it is widely perceived as 'other'. This, too, is something discussed in the pages that follow, together with how our perception of the sea has shaped Christian thought and spirituality as well as more ancient religious and philosophical traditions that Christianity has drawn upon, including Platonism and Celtic nature worship.

While exploring the influence of the sea on Christianity involves venturing into uncharted waters, even a cursory reading of the Bible makes it clear that the sea plays an important role in the story of salvation that runs through it as a continuous thread. From the stories of creation, the Flood, and the crossing of the Red Sea in the Book of Genesis, to the exploits of Jonah, the trials of Job, the apocalyptic visions of Daniel, the miracles of Jesus, the missionary journeys of Paul, and the vision of the new Jerusalem in the Book of Revelation, the literal or symbolic presence of the sea is crucial. In fact, as will be suggested, the biblical narrative of creation, fall, redemption, and the vision of re-creation in the end times cannot be fully explained without reference to the sea, such was its significance in the thought-world of the 1,300 year period during which the books of the Bible were written.

Shaping the biblical imagery of the sea are the experiences of generations who have encountered it in ways best described as 'spiritual'. What was the case for ancient civilizations has also been true throughout history and continues today. Consequently, the 'spirituality' of the sea is rich and varied. As will be seen, the sea has provided the context for an important strand of Christian asceticism and monasticism, particularly in the Celtic rim of Western Europe, elements of which have been resurgent in recent years through the growing interest in Celtic Christianity.

The sea has been used by numerous theologians and spiritual writers who have gleaned from their own experiences images and metaphors for expressing what is ultimately inexpressible – the nature of God. The sea has also inspired generations of artists, poets, novelists, playwrights, musicians, and film-makers who have found its varying moods not only fascinating but an impulse for creativity, often with religious connotations. The sea's mysterious depths have fascinated psychologists, who see parallels with the human psyche and perhaps even the soul. Those who live on the coast speak, too, of the profound spiritual effect the sea has on them, as do those who go to sea for work or leisure, as their lives straddle safe and familiar surroundings on land and unknown and dangerous elemental waters. Exploring how... sea has been interpreted within Christianity therefore requires looking closely at this broader spiritual dimension as well.

The importance of spirituality as a tool for theological enquiry is now widely recognised, having long been treated with suspicion because of appearing irrational; that is, because of its association with emotional feelings. If theology is regarded as an intellectual, scholarly pursuit, then spirituality is seen more as experiential. Yet it is only by examining the wide range of experiences of our interaction with the sea that we can understand the sense of 'otherness' that it evokes, an evocation which underlies the biblical texts and subsequent theological reflection. And so this book draws from a wide and varied range of sources across history, including not only the work of biblical scholars and theologians, but sailors, travel writers, oceanographers, marine biologists, geographers, psychologists, and psychiatrists, as well as the accounts of many others who have recorded having religious or spiritual encounters with the sea.

The lure of the sea is a fascinating area of enquiry. So, too, is the study of the social and geo-political contexts within which the Christian story unfolds. The sea has helped shape nations, communities, individuals, and their beliefs. Cultures are often defined not so much by political boundaries but by those that are natural, such as coastlines. Thus, it is possible to speak of the Mediterranean not only as a sea but as a region where people of different countries, languages, and religions share much in common because of the way they interact with the water around which they live. As will be seen, this regional dimension was especially important for the development of Christianity as it spread from its roots in the Middle East.

From a British perspective, being an 'island nation' – or more accurately an archipelago – has many implications, some of which are shared by other such countries. For millennia, the sea has formed a border across which invaders and missionaries have ventured. It has provided a means of transport and communication around the British Isles and further afield. The sea has been a natural defence barrier from armed invasion and diseases such as rabies, a source of food, a battlefield, and a playground. The sea helps determine indigenous wildlife, such as the absence of snakes from Ireland, as well as shape climate, and therefore flora and fauna. Perhaps, too, the psychological effect of the separation by water of England, Northern Ireland, Scotland, and Wales from mainland Europe may partly explain the outcome of the 2016 referendum on membership of the European Union.

Britain's place in world history, including its role in the Christian mission, has been greatly influenced by phases of maritime supremacy. This is apparent in one of the most influential religious works in the English language, *The Book of Common Prayer*. Archbishop Thomas Cranmer's 1662 *Prayer Book*, which is a formative text throughout the Anglican Communion (and, of course, first disseminated across the world by sea), contains 'Forms of Prayer to be Used at Sea'. Significantly longer than the section on marriage, it includes daily prayers for the navy; prayers for use during storms, before and after a battle, and for the enemy; various thanksgivings following storms and tempest, and an order for burial at sea. Interestingly, when the *Prayer Book* was due to be revised in 1928 these prayers were left intact, while the more recent *Alternative Service Book 1980* and *Common Worship* of 2000 contain no modern language equivalents.

A growing area of academic research is the study of 'place': how we interpret locations, how we interact with our surroundings, and how the resulting sense of place shapes our personal and cultural identity. Studies crossing the boundaries of anthropology, geography, and sociology have spawned the new discipline of 'geosophy', to which contributions have been made recently by theologians such as David Brown, John Inge, and Philip Sheldrake. It has long been the case that people have been drawn to particular locations for religious reasons, and certainly in Britain and Ireland many sacred sites are by the sea. George McLeod, founder of the modern Iona community, famously described the island of Iona on the west coast of Scotland as a 'thin place', where the boundary between Earth and Heaven seems porous. Others would say the same of Holy Island (Lindisfarne) on the Northumberland coast; Bardsey Island, the supposed burial site of 'twenty thousand saints' off the Llyn Peninsula of north-west Wales; and Skellig Michael, the dramatic monastic settlement – and now UNESCO World Heritage Site and *Star Wars* set – off the Dingle Peninsula of south-west Ireland. This notion of the 'thin place' will also be explored in the pages that follow.

Living on the edge of land and sea is a formative experience for many people across the world. In Britain, with its 19,000 or so miles of coastline, many lives have been shaped by the sight, sound, and smell of the sea, and its changing temperament. A significant question for those interested in the theology of place is how God is mediated by a particular location. There is a deep truth in Carol Ann Duffy's poem 'Prayer' that reflects on how familiar places and experiences can have a spiritual dimension – even listening to the shipping forecast: 'Darkness outside. Inside, the radio's prayer – / Rockall. Malin. Finisterre.' A Christian understanding of place may be expressed in many ways, including local customs, liturgies, hymns, church dedications and decorations, and there is much to explore here from the perspective of those who live by the sea. Again, this is something this book explores.

Despite Britain's rich maritime heritage, popular awareness of the sea has diminished considerably in recent decades. This has much to do with the vast growth of air travel and, more recently, the opening of the Channel Tunnel. Since the first half of the twentieth century it has been possible to leave mainland Britain in ways other than by sea. These, together with the downsizing of the navy, the collapse of a once significant shipbuilding industry, the decline of fisheries, and the decreased popularity of British seaside resorts have all contributed to a reduced awareness of the sea that surrounds us. Perhaps Britain's most important maritime activity today is decidedly land-based and hidden from public view. Through Lloyd's of London and the Baltic Exchange, the City remains the world's main centre for marine insurance and the hub of international shipping. Yet these important service industries are no longer located cheek-by-jowl with the great centre of trade from which they emerged. The Port of London today is a shadow of its former self, when it was at the heart of international commerce.

National awareness of the sea in Britain has diminished significantly since the Second World War. Not only was it widely recognised during the war that the sea provided a final defence against invasion, but public consciousness of the dependence on sea travel was intensified when the German navy attempted to starve Britain and stop imports of armaments and other vital equipment. This posed a severe threat and was an important factor behind the introduction of rationing, affecting the daily lives of everyone. Public attention was focused on shipping and what Winston Churchill termed 'the Battle of the Atlantic'. In this conflict, which Churchill said was 'the only thing that ever frightened me', over 5,000 allied ships were sunk and 100,000 lives lost on both sides. It was a time of acute awareness – both positive and negative – of being an island nation. For the post-war generations such awareness has all but vanished, although the grounding of aircraft across Europe in 2010 because of the spread of ash from the Eyjafjallajökull volcano in Iceland gave a temporary reminder, when stranded travellers returned *en masse* to Britain on crowded ships.

If the sea is no longer in the forefront of our minds, it still surrounds us and remains vitally important to our existence. Over 90 per cent of international trade is transported at sea, and the English Channel remains one of the world's busiest routes for commercial shipping. Much of what we eat, wear, and use will have travelled perhaps thousands of miles across water, on ships crewed by sailors whose daily lives are significantly different from those of us who live on land. Furthermore, advances in technology allow us to search beneath the sea or sea-bed for resources and to exploit its power. As we have become more aware of the finitude of the Earth's resources, the sea and sea-bed have come increasingly to our attention as we seek new sources of raw materials and energy. We are interacting with the marine environment in new ways, as we pit our entrepreneurial spirit, ingenuity, and insatiable appetite for economic growth against the natural challenges the sea poses.

What is bringing the sea back into our consciousness most of all, however, is not the opportunities it offers, but the threats it poses and faces. The large number of fatalities among migrants trying to cross the Mediterranean in over-crowded or unseaworthy boats is a disturbing reminder of the dangers of being at sea, and of how the most vulnerable people are often those most at risk. The shocking and heart-breaking photograph of a soldier carrying the body of three year-old Alan Kurdi, which had been washed up on a Turkish beach in September 2015 after his family tried to flee the war in Syria, will surely be one of the defining images of the early twenty-first century.

In contrast to horrific pictures of human suffering, the BBC television series *Blue Planet II* used stunning visual imagery to highlight the devastating impact of ocean plastic pollution on marine life and the food chain, and has helped champion campaigns to reduce plastic waste. While pollution poses one threat, climate change is causing sea levels to rise, putting low-lying coastal areas and delta regions and their populations at risk. It is hard to project accurately the likely extent of rising sea levels in the twenty-first century. The complexity of analysing the combined effects of the thermal expansion of seawater and the rate of melting glaciers, ice-caps, and ice-sheets means we cannot be sure what will happen in the long run, and much of the data and its analysis remain controversial. What is incontrovertible, however, is that sea levels are rising. If they rise by 83cm over the remainder of this century, as many predict, this would be enough to cause devastation to low-lying places such as Bangladesh and the Maldives, and put the Netherlands, and even London, in danger. It is salutary to note that the Thames Barrier, London's sea defence, was closed 182 times between 1983, when it came into operation, and February 2018 – 95 times to protect against tidal flooding and 87 times to protect against combined tidal and fluvial (river) flooding, with 50 closures in 2013-14 alone.

As a result of climate change, the sea is beginning to re-emerge in the public consciousness in ways akin to the biblical perceptions of threat and danger. Startling images from around the world of flood damage, coupled with increased awareness of the impact of rising sea levels around coastlines, are having an impact. Not only are they rekindling a sense of awe and wonder of the waters that presently cover over 70 per cent of the Earth's surface and account for over 95 per cent of its environment that can sustain life, but they are also reminding us of the sea's destructiveness and our inability to control its immense power. We are living in what is termed the 'Anthropocene', a geological age for which there is overwhelming scientific evidence that human activity is having an unprecedented impact on the environment. The fact that humans are responsible for climate change means that today's rising sea levels call to mind the story of the Flood and of divine judgment on humanity. An ancient myth is re-emerging as a timeless myth, and those of us who have lost awareness of the sea and its devastating power are becoming conscious of it in a disturbing way, sharing with our neighbours in coastal regions and islands across the 'Blue Planet' a renewed sense of the sea's presence.

In the light of this returning awareness of the waters that surround us, this book seeks to articulate what is often felt but seldom put into words: how we interact with the sea, not so much physically (though that is part of it) but spiritually, from the perspective of religious faith. The task before us is to put this into the bigger picture of two millennia of Christianity, and finally to offer a contemporary theological and spiritual response to this interaction. To do this, we begin by exploring the role the sea plays in the Bible – first in the Hebrew scriptures of the Old Testament, and then in the specifically Christian scriptures of the New Testament. In the process we will discover that in this remarkable and diverse collection of 66 books it is possible to discern a continuous thread that stretches from Genesis to Revelation in which the sea plays a vital role.

From biblical times we move into the early centuries of Christianity, as the faith was spread by sea travel and stretched the minds of those whose world-view was shaped by their encounters with the sea. This takes us on to consider the arrival, by sea, of Christianity to the British Isles, and the development of monasticism and the distinctive way it was shaped by coastal and island locations. From there, we consider how the 'age of discovery' changed perceptions of the sea and geography from a religious perspective, as did later advances in science. The impact of social change in the eighteenth century is also considered as a factor in altering attitudes towards the sea. This then leads us to consider the association of the sea with religious experience, and finally its sacramental nature.

This is an ambitious sweep, and if this book can be likened to a ship's log, it is more akin to a log for a voyage of discovery than for a cruise to a well-known destination. Taking the analogy one step further, the point of departure for a voyage is often safe and familiar, and so it is here. Any theological study of the sea must take into account one of the best known pieces of religious literature: the story of creation in the opening passage of the Book of Genesis, and it is from here that the voyage begins.

1   Joseph Conrad, *The Nigger of the Narcissus* (New York: Doubleday, 1914), p. 47.
2   F.W. Dillistone, *Christianity and Symbolism*, (London: Collins, 1955), p. 15.

1

The Deep

The idea of 'the Deep' is so powerful that if we listen
to the word as we say it a shiver may pass through
in recognition of all the associations it has jarred
into resonance.

James Hamilton-Paterson,
Seven Tenths: The Sea and its Thresholds

'In the beginning, when God created the heavens and the earth, the earth
was a formless void and darkness covered the face of the deep, while a wind
swept over the face of the waters' (Genesis 1:1-2). With these sonorous
words the Jewish Bible begins and so also the Christian story of creation,
fall, and salvation. It is where this book begins as well, for there can be no
better starting place for an exploration of the sea in Christian thinking and
spirituality.

The opening of Genesis is familiar to believers and non-believers alike.
It is loved for its mysterious beauty and evocation of an existence before the
dawn of time. It has also become controversial, and widely debated by those
working at the interface of science and religion. Yet, despite its familiarity, it
says something that is all too easily overlooked. It describes the original state
from which the cosmos is created as a vast expanse of *water*: 'the deep' (*t^{e}hōm*
in Hebrew). Earth is a formless void – nothing – but there is substance in the
form of a primordial ocean. It is an image rarely commented on in the vast
and varied literature where Genesis is mentioned.

What is also significant is that nowhere in Genesis does it say 'God created
the deep'. According to Genesis, before creation takes place there is darkness
and a void (so there is no light or solid elemental material) but there is water,
the surface of which is agitated by the Spirit of God as if by wind. There is
no suggestion here of God creating the deep *ex nihilo* (out of nothing); that

is a later concept in both Christianity and Judaism. If anything, this passage is suggestive of the deep as eternal, co-existing with God.

The opening of Genesis should be regarded neither as a scientific description of creation nor a creation myth, but rather as a statement of faith about the relationship between the Creator and creation. The point of this is to say – clearly and boldly – that the God of Israel is in total control of the cosmos. The choice of symbolism is significant. Underlying the Genesis story is a profound sense that this primordial ocean lies mysteriously outside what was understood as the created order. The deep is something 'other': it is the pre-creation chaos out of which God brings order to create the cosmos. The deep therefore represents what is otherwise uncontrollable and untameable. The theological point being made is that if the God of Israel is able to tame and control this primordial chaos, then that God is truly omnipotent.

This powerful image of 'the deep' lies at the heart of the Judaeo-Christian understanding of the sea. As Genesis goes on to describe, it is from the parting of the deep that 'the waters that cover the earth' – seas, lakes, and rivers – are formed. In Genesis, these vast expanses of water are seen as the tamed part of the primordial chaos that bring a strong sense of timeless 'otherness' into our ordered everyday existence. Similar ideas are found in creation stories elsewhere, and it is almost certain that ancient Israelites drew from those of neighbouring religions and cultures and wove into them a distinctive Jewish theology. What distinguishes the Genesis story from others is that it portrays God as purposeful, and firmly and serenely in control. In contrast, Ugaritic, Babylonian, and other Middle Eastern stories speak of the creation of the Earth as almost an accidental by-product of a violent cosmic battle involving sea gods. More akin to the calmer, deliberate Jewish understanding of creation is that found in Islam, where the Koran describes the throne of God as being upon water. Similarly, in the creation story in Hinduism, the divine swan Hamsa, swimming on primordial waters, hatches the golden egg of the Earth. This explains why, in India, the divine presence is sometimes symbolised by a lotus leaf floating on water.

In a similar vein, stories parallel to that of Noah and the Flood found in Genesis are also widespread across religions, sharing the theme that humanity is punished and purged of its sinfulness by a divinely ordained flood. Such narratives are found in Islam, Hinduism, Zoroastrianism, and religions of the Far East; among the ancient stories of the indigenous people of Australia, the first nation peoples of North America, Mayan and Aztec cultures in South America, and communities in Hawaii and other Pacific islands; and in Scandinavian, pre-Christian Celtic, and classical Greco-Roman mythology.

Of course, it is possible that some of these stories developed independently, as peoples in different parts of the world sought to make sense of their experiences of devastating floods through the lens of their religious beliefs. It is also likely that the kernel of the story was transmitted across some religions and cultures.

There is certainly a striking similarity between the story of the Flood found in Genesis and that in the much earlier Babylonian *Epic of Gilgamesh*, which was discovered on clay tablets by the English archaeologist and politician Austen Henry Layard in 1839, during an excavation of the ancient city of Nineveh in what is now Iraq. The *Epic of Gilgamesh* is generally regarded as the oldest surviving significant work of literature, probably dating from the third millennium BCE, and its parallels with the much later biblical story of the Flood are striking. In *Gilgamesh*, the Mesopotamian gods are so displeased with the noise of humans that they decide to exterminate them all. However, Ea, the god of wisdom and one of the creators of humans, succeeds in saving one good person, Utnapishtim, telling him in a dream to build a boat and take with him the 'the seed' of all living creatures. After obeying this instruction, Utnapishtim, his family, and all creatures on board are saved from a devastating flood, with the boat settling on a mountaintop from which Utnapishtim sends out a dove. Given that *Gilgamesh* predates the story of Noah by at least a thousand years, it is hard not to believe that it lies behind the biblical Flood narrative.

What is immediately striking about Genesis and related Middle Eastern texts is how negatively the sea is portrayed: it is both chaotic (the deep) and destructive (the Flood). The more celebratory way water is generally perceived in religions throws this negativity towards the sea into sharp contrast. Water holds a special place in Islam, for example. The Koran states that water is the source of all life, with every living thing made from it. Perhaps there is a link here with Genesis, and the idea that the deep pre-exists created matter. Also, for Muslim pilgrims on Hajj or Umrah to Mecca, a required ritual is to drink from the Zamzam well which, according to Islamic belief, sprang up miraculously on the spot where the thirsty infant Ishmael stamped his foot. The Bible, too, speaks frequently of the life-giving properties of water. Springs, wells, and fountains of 'living water' and the 'waters of life' appear in the Song of Songs, the prophecies of Jeremiah and Zechariah, John's gospel, and the Book of Revelation.

Some of the positive biblical references to water are metaphorical, referring not only to the importance of water for sustaining life but to what refreshes people spiritually. This imagery is used to powerful effect in John's gospel.

Here, the gospel writer uses the wonderful story of the wedding at Cana, where water is turned into wine, as a sign of Jesus' transforming presence, heralding the coming of God's kingdom. The setting of a wedding feast is appropriate, for a traditional image of the Kingdom of God in Jewish thought is that of a great banquet. Later in the same gospel, Jesus' conversation with the Samaritan woman at Jacob's well (John 4:14) leads to the use of the symbolism of 'living water' as representing eternal life, which is open to Jews and Gentiles alike – including the despised Samaritans.

In many religions, water is valued because of its cleansing properties. This is particularly so in Hinduism where the river Ganges, which flows from the Himalayas (the mountains of the gods), is of special significance. Some Hindus believe that there is an imperative to bathe at least once in a lifetime in the Ganges. For centuries, holy springs and wells were widespread within Christianity, often at sites that were sacred to pre-Christian religions. This can be seen today through place-names such as Holywell in North Wales or Wells, the cathedral city in Somerset. Some pilgrim sites associated with water, such as Lourdes, remain important today as places of healing, drawing on ideas associated with water's cleansing and life-giving properties. This is not surprising, given the importance of potable water for sustaining life. When St Francis of Assisi wrote in his 'Canticle of the Sun', 'Praised be thou, O Lord, for sister water, who is very useful, humble, precious and chaste', it was a significant prayer of thanksgiving, as pure (chaste) water was vital for survival, something too easily forgotten for those of us accustomed to safe water supplies – though not for the 1.1 billion in the world today for whom water-borne disease is an everyday threat.

Water, too, is found as a symbol for the soul, no doubt because of its association with life and because of its mysterious, fluid properties and quixotic ability to evaporate into gas. As Goethe's 'Song of the Spirits over the Water' puts it:

> The spirit of Man
> Resembles water:
> Coming from heaven,
> Rising to heaven,
> And hither and thither,
> To Earth must then
> Ever descend.

The nineteenth-century German philosopher and anthropologist, Ludwig Feuerbach, who turned away from the Church to become an atheist and arch-critic of Christianity, argued that God was an outward projection of our inner nature. He nevertheless recognised the symbolic potency of water. In his stinging critique of Christian sacraments in *The Essence of Christianity* Feuerbach wrote of the role of water in baptism (with the help of his English translator, George Eliot):

> Water is the purest, clearest of liquids; in virtue of this its natural character it is the image of the spotless nature of the Divine Spirit. In short, water has a significance of itself, as water; it is on account of its natural quality that it is consecrated and selected as the vehicle of the Holy Spirit.[1]

Interestingly, the Bible makes no clear distinction between freshwater and seawater. Although seawater is undrinkable (to the torment of Coleridge's parched Ancient Mariner), it was nevertheless an important source of food in the Middle East. Sea-fishing provided a plentiful food supply, while salt, an important food preservative, was obtained by the evaporation of seawater and from the cliffs of the world's saltiest sea, the Dead Sea. Called the Salt Sea in the Bible, the mineral-laden Dead Sea was also known in biblical times for its health-giving properties. Together, these factors suggest that the negative image of the sea in the Bible is more to do with its wild, unpredictable nature than because it is undrinkable.

This emphasis on wildness is apparent in Genesis, where there is an implicit distinction between 'sea' and 'ocean'. As already mentioned, the ocean is associated with primordial chaos – it is what was left over after the sea, lakes, and rivers were created. This distinction owes much to geography of the region where Judaism emerged. The ancient Israelites' understanding of the marine environment was shaped by their knowledge and experience, which came primarily from navigation in and around the Mediterranean. There is a sense of this in Psalm 107, a thanksgiving for deliverance from troubles:

> Some went down to the sea in ships,
> doing business on the mighty waters;
> they saw the deeds of the Lord,
> his wondrous works in the deep.
> For he commanded and raised the stormy wind,
> which lifted up the waves of the sea.
> They mounted up to heaven, they went down to the depths;
> their courage melted away in their calamity;
> they reeled and staggered like drunkards,

and were at their wits' end.
Then they cried to the Lord in their trouble,
and he brought them out from their distress;
he made the storm be still,
and the waves of the sea were hushed.

(Psalm 107:23-29)

Sailors of the time (as of today) were acutely aware of the considerable difference between the relatively calm, safe, and tide-less waters of the Mediterranean, and the wild, dangerous, and tidal waters of the Atlantic. This distinction is most clearly expressed in Classical mythology (also the product of a Mediterranean society) in which the Pillars of Hercules – the European and North African promontories at the entrance of the Strait of Gibraltar – provide not only a significant physical boundary between sea and ocean, but a spiritual boundary as well. Also known as the Gates of Hades, the Pillars of Hercules were perceived by the ancient Greeks as the entrance to the underworld, such was the association between the ocean and death and the unknown.

So although both sea and ocean are components of the biblical deep, there was a qualitative difference between the two in the minds of ancient Middle Eastern and Mediterranean peoples. For Greeks, Romans, Jews, and others, the untamed ocean was much closer to the chaotic state and to 'other worlds' than was the more orderly, placid sea. The sea is what God had created; the ocean is a remnant of the pre-creation, chaotic deep. As will be seen, this distinction persisted for centuries, influencing Christian attitudes until explorers (including Christian missionaries) pushed the boundaries of the world as known by Western Europeans and others beyond the Atlantic and changed our understanding of the Earth's geography. More prosaically, it also means that where a distinction between ocean and sea has to be made in this book, the different terms will be used. Otherwise 'sea' will be used in its generic sense to mean both.

Although the Bible is a collection of diverse books written in different contexts over hundreds of years, it is possible to discern a narrative thread that runs throughout, quite literally from Genesis to Revelation. The thread is the story of salvation; of God making right something that has gone wrong with humanity and our relationship with God. The sea plays a key role in this story.

The Bible opens with the creation of the Earth and its creatures. The need for salvation quickly emerges because of the fall of humanity through our wilful disobedience of God. The process of salvation begins when God judges humanity and seeks to purge us of sin by the Flood, leaving only a faithful remnant from which a renewed human race can emerge. The theme continues with God establishing a special, covenantal relationship with his chosen people, the Israelites, who are to be a 'light to the nations' offering the hope of salvation to all; and much of the Hebrews' scriptures describe their struggle to stay faithful to the covenant. For Christians, the story extends into the New Testament with the saving acts of Jesus Christ and ends in the Book of Revelation with a hopeful eschatological image of a perfected new creation made possible by the salvation achieved by Jesus' life, death, resurrection, and ascension. The sea plays an important role throughout this narrative thread, and it is from this, and in particular the sea's association with chaos, that many of its negative theological connotations derive.

The divine act of creation brings order out of chaos. We are told that on the second day of creation, 'the firmament' is put in place by divine command. In the thought-world of the time, the firmament was seen as a great hemisphere placed within the waters of the deep, separating the waters that were now above and below the firmament. Then, on the third day of creation, the waters below are drained away to expose dry land. The land was imagined as a solid disc resting upon, and surrounded by, the primal waters: what we understand as ocean. But there is another ocean. Above the firmament is the heavenly ocean, the blueness of which could be seen from below, and which from time to time would water the Earth through a lattice or windows with rain, snow, and hail (see Figure 1). Within this thought-world, where the oceans above and below can reconnect, the return to chaos is an ever-present threat. As Gerhard von Rad put it:

> Man has always suspected that behind all creation lies the abyss of formlessness, further, that all creation is always ready to sink into the abyss of the formless, that the chaos therefore signifies simply the threat to everything created, and this suspicion has been a constant temptation for his faith.[2]

The destructive force at work that pushes humanity towards chaos is understood to be sinfulness; our disobedience of God. Chaos is therefore closely associated with evil and distancing from God. What prevents the retreat to chaos from happening is God's will. It is almost possible to summarise the Bible as a description of the tension between these two competing forces: of how God's will is done despite our best efforts to stifle it, from the disobedience of Adam and Eve in the Garden of Eden to crucifying Christ. From a theological perspective the current environmental crisis, which appears to be largely the consequence of human behaviour, can be seen in terms of a damaged relationship with the Creator.

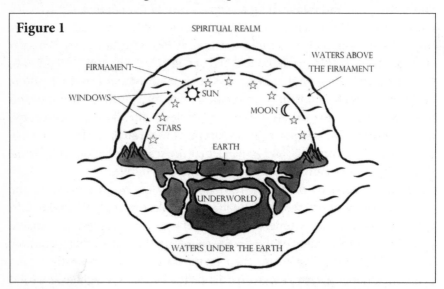

Figure 1

Biblical scholars date the opening account of creation in Genesis as having been written sometime between the eighth century BCE and the Israelites' exile in Babylon, which began in 586/7 BCE. They attribute it to the 'Priestly' school of theology, which emphasised monotheism and well-ordered religious practices. A shorthand description for Priestly theology might be 'Yahweh (God) is in control and is orderly.' The other creation story in Genesis, that of Paradise and Adam and Eve, is thought to be much older and the product of the 'Yahwist' school of theology, which operated around the tenth or ninth century BCE. It describes how, when humans are created, they quickly become rebellious and disobedient to God. In chapters 6 to 9, fallen humanity comes under God's judgment, and God's response is dramatic and almost indiscriminate: God allows a brief return to the chaotic state before creation. Only Noah, his family, and a representative group of creatures escape the devastation.

Like the opening stories of Genesis, the story of the Flood also comes from a mixture of the Priestly and Yahwistic sources. The Priestly account speaks of the heavenly ocean emptying itself down, and of the water below being freed of its bonds, so that for a time the two sections of the primal ocean are reunited. In other words, God wills that, briefly, chaos reigns once more to purge the world of sinfulness. When this purging ends, the Priestly story tells of God entering into a covenant with Noah to establish a new relationship between God and humanity. The covenant is famously symbolised by a rainbow: a symbol of a giant bow of war across the sky, as light refracts through water droplets. In this covenant, God has set aside this watery weapon, which points away from the Earth.

The weapon is set aside but not forgotten. There is a clear echo of the Flood in Exodus in the story of the Israelites' escape from bondage in Egypt and their journey through the wilderness towards freedom in the Promised Land. To get there they must cross the Red Sea. Again, there is a mixture of source material in this story. In the Priestly account, Moses is given power by God to part the sea so that the Israelites can cross on dry land; and he is also given the power to let the sea return to its normal state and destroy the pursuing Egyptians as they try to cross. God, through Moses, is firmly in control. In their study of the sea in the Bible, Srokosz and Watson describe this event as 'the pivotal moment of faith and salvation.'[3] It was by passing through the Red Sea and eventually entering into the Promised Land that Israel was saved and established as the people of God.

The reason the sea plays such an important role in the Hebrew scriptures probably has much to do with the real experience of flooding in various parts of North Africa and the Middle East over centuries, passed down in stories from generation to generation. The sea was beyond human control and understood to bring about chaos, death, and destruction by the action of God or gods. Not surprisingly, it was therefore associated with sin and evil. As well as being dangerous itself, the sea is portrayed in the Bible as the home of mysterious creatures or monsters. Perhaps this came out of genuine accounts of attacks by sharks or of boats being upturned by surfacing whales, or of strange creatures caught by fishermen or washed up on beaches. The great sense of not knowing what existed in the sea's depths undoubtedly fuelled fear and intrigue, helping to create the mythical sea monsters such as the biblical Leviathan and Rahab, or Scylla in Greek mythology.

The 'monsters of the deep' mostly provide fearful images in the Bible, but there are two exceptions. Psalm 104 provides a beautiful image of creation, and because it predates the Priestly account of creation in Genesis, it is generally thought to have influenced Genesis. Describing what takes place in and on the sea, the psalmist says, 'There go the ships, and Leviathan that you formed to sport in it' (verse 26). This monster appears here as God's plaything. This benign image of the sea monster is famously used to powerful effect in the Book of Jonah. Unlike other prophetic books, Jonah is not a collection of prophecies but the story of a prophet. It tells of how the reluctant prophet Jonah is called by God to prophesy to the sinful inhabitants of the city of Nineveh. Jonah's immediate response is to reject God's call, and to escape by going to sea, sailing from Joppa to Tarshish – that is from the modern-day port of Jaffa to what is thought to be the ancient Greek city Tartessos, a Phoenician colony in southern Spain, which in the Hebrew mind-set was at the edge of the world.

The story of Jonah uses the twin images of the sea and sea monster to demonstrate God's total control of the situation. First of all, Jonah cannot escape from God, whose presence is made known by creating a storm. Jonah offers to save those on board ship by throwing himself into the chaotic waters in the hope that his self-sacrifice will appease God and restore calm. Jonah is saved by being swallowed alive and spewed out by a giant fish. God's total control of the situation is demonstrated again by the fact that even what would otherwise be regarded as a fearful sea monster submits to God's will, and by doing so becomes an instrument of salvation. A distinctly disgruntled Jonah then goes on to deliver his prophecy to the people of Nineveh: 'Forty days more, and Nineveh shall be overthrown!' (Jonah 3:4). These eight words cause the people of Nineveh to repent and they are saved from destruction – which makes Jonah even more disgruntled, as he believes they deserve punishment.

So how did this fearful image of the sea and its monsters come to be in the Bible? The nineteenth-century biblical scholar Herman Gunkel argued that the Bible was influenced by Mediterranean and Near Eastern mythology and proposed that the Priestly account of creation in Genesis draws heavily from the Babylonian creation myth.[4] It has been argued that the Hebrew word for 'the deep', *tᵉhōm*, is related to the name of the Babylonian goddess of the sea, Tiamet. In the Babylonian creation epic *Enûma Elish* Tiamet is, in the words of the science fiction writer-cum-theologian Isaac Asimov, 'as wild, as lawless, as powerful as the sea.'[5] Tiamet is killed by the storm-god Marduk in a great cosmic battle, and it is from her carcass, sliced in half, that Heaven and Earth are formed – an image similar to the dividing of the waters in Genesis. Where the parallel ends is that in Genesis there is no suggestion of a struggle – the almighty God has total control over the deep.

Despite the possible link between *tᵉhōm* and Tiamet, it is now more generally thought that the story on which the Genesis account is based is not the Babylonian myth but a similar Canaanite story, which would have been more local to ancient Israelites following their settlement in Canaan. This change in understanding followed the discovery of texts in the ancient Canaanite port of Ugarit (known today as Ras Shamra) on the Mediterranean coast in the 1920s. Although the Canaanite story is not about creation, it is about a battle for divine control of the cosmos in which the power of chaos, represented by sea-god Yamm, is overcome by the god Baal. Whichever story influenced Genesis, what is significant is that throughout the Middle East the sea was regarded as symbolising chaos and was woven into, and absorbed by, the mythology of several cultures. This points to an ancient and universal fascination with the sea, a widespread mistrust of it, and a pervasive sense of its 'otherness'.

The influence of the Canaanite story of Baal and Yamm on the Hebrew scriptures has been explored by John Day, who sees evidence of the idea of a battle at the time of creation particularly in the Psalms, such as Psalm 74:

> Yet God my King is from of old,
> working salvation in the earth.
> You divided the sea by your might;
> you broke the heads of the dragons in the water.
> You crushed the Leviathan;
> you gave him as food for the creatures of the wilderness. [6]
>
> (Psalm 74:12-14)

Day also suggests that this battle lies behind much of the sea imagery in references to creation in the Book of Job. In this remarkable exploration of why good people suffer, as the faithful and suffering Job seeks to make sense of his predicament he grapples to understand the nature of God. Job describes God as having 'trampled the waves of the Sea' (9:8) and who 'By his power he stilled the Sea; by his understanding he struck down Rahab' (26:12). Both images suggest God has overcome hostile forces, rather than having absolute, serene control as in the Priestly school of thought.

Yet elsewhere in Job there is a very different portrayal of the sea, much more in line with Priestly theology. Towards the end of the book, God responds to Job and the response includes a description of God's control of the sea at creation that likens it to a birth:

> who shut in the sea with doors
> when it burst out from the womb? –
> when I made the clouds its garment,
> and thick darkness its swaddling band,

> and prescribed bounds for it,
> and set bars and doors,
> and said, 'Thus far shall you come and no farther,
> and here shall your proud waves be stopped.'
>
> (Job 38:8-11)

Day also highlights how the menacing sea or sea monster is used as an image to represent nations that were hostile to Israel. In Isaiah, for instance, those that 'thunder like the thundering of the sea!' (17:12) probably refers to Assyria, whose empire dominated the Middle East in the ninth to seventh centuries BCE, while Habakkuk's phrase 'You trampled the sea with your horses, churning the mighty waters' (3:15) refers to Babylon, which was responsible for the destruction of Jerusalem and the taking of Israelites into captivity in 587 BCE.

The use of the sea to represent hostility towards Israel is also apparent in the Psalms, although these references are difficult to relate to specific threats. Psalm 144, for example, could include a prayer for help in many situations of conflict:

> Stretch out your hand from on high;
> set me free and rescue me from the mighty waters,
> from the hand of aliens,
> whose mouths speak lies,
> and whose right hands are false.
>
> (Psalm 144:7-8)

In all, 32 psalms refer to the sea. While the use of the sea as a metaphor for enemies is common in them, even more pronounced are two other themes. Fourteen psalms refer to the sea to express something of God's majesty and control over nature. It is thought that many of these originated in an ancient New Year festival in which Yahweh was 'enthroned' as king of the universe. Psalm 24 is one of these:

> The earth is the Lord's and all that is in it,
> the world, and those who live in it;
> for he has founded it on the seas,
> and established it on the rivers.
>
> (Psalm 24:1-2)

Similarly, Psalm 29 speaks of God's kingship in terms of control of water:

> The Lord is enthroned over the flood;

the Lord is enthroned as king for ever.
May the Lord give strength to his people!
May the Lord bless his people with peace!
(Psalm 29:10-11)

God's enthronement as king of the universe was represented symbolically in the architecture of the First Temple in Jerusalem. Also known as Solomon's Temple, it was structured and decorated to be, in Margaret Barker's words, 'the microcosm of the whole creation' overseen by God's throne in the Holy of Holies.[7] The First Book of Kings describes how King Solomon employed Hiram, who was skilled in working in bronze, to produce metalwork for the temple, including a giant representation of the sea:

> Then he made the cast sea; it was round, ten cubits from brim to brim, and five cubits high. A line of thirty cubits would encircle it completely. Under its brim were panels all round it, each of ten cubits, surrounding the sea; there were two rows of panels, cast when it was cast. It stood on twelve oxen, three facing north, three facing west, three facing south, and three facing east; the sea was set on them. The hindquarters of each were towards the inside. Its thickness was a handbreadth; its brim was made like the brim of a cup, like the flower of a lily; it held two thousand baths.
>
> (1 Kings 7:23-26)

The other recurring theme in the Psalms that refer to the sea is that of salvation. There are numerous references to the chosen people being saved by the parting of the Red Sea in thanksgiving psalms, as well as the threat of the sea being used in psalms that are prayers for deliverance. An example is Psalm 66:

> Come and see what God has done:
> he is awesome in his deeds among mortals.
> He turned the sea into dry land;
> they passed through the river on foot.
> There we rejoiced in him,
> who rules by his might for ever,
> whose eyes keep watch on the nations—
> let the rebellious not exalt themselves.
>
> (Psalm 66:5-7)

If the biblical story of salvation begins with the creation, then it concludes with what will be in the 'end times' – what theologians refer to as 'eschatology'. There are numerous eschatological passages in the Hebrew scriptures, and again the sea features prominently. Psalm 46:2-3 gives a vivid image of the tumult during the last days when 'the earth should change' and 'mountains shake in the heart of the sea', and 'its waters roar and foam.' Isaiah 27:1 prophesies concerning the end times when, 'On that day the Lord with his cruel and great and strong sword will punish Leviathan the fleeing serpent, Leviathan the twisting serpent, and he will kill the dragon that is in the sea.' Daniel 7:1-12 contains an apocalyptic vision of the end times. The prophet dreams of 'the four great winds of heaven stirring up the great sea', and of how 'four great beasts came up out of the sea'. The vision continues with the enthronement of 'the Ancient One' who sits in judgement while the most terrifying of the sea-monsters is put to death and the others taken away, their lives prolonged 'for a season and a day.' These horrific images of the defeat of sea monsters are used to show that in the end times, when God's reign is complete, the forces of evil will be overcome.

The sea, then, plays a significant role in the Hebrew scriptures. The writers and editors of these ancient holy texts drew on stories common across the Middle East and infused them with a distinctive Jewish understanding of God. While the omnipotent Creator can control even the primordial waters of chaos, what remains beyond control is humanity. Imbued with free-will, humanity abuses this God-given gift and is therefore in need of salvation. The salvation of humanity is a recurring theme throughout the Hebrew scriptures and, for Christians, continues in the New Testament. As we will see, here, too, the sea plays a central role.

1   Ludwig Feuerbach (trans. George Eliot), *The Essence of Christianity* (New York: Cosimo, 2008), p. 237.
2   Gerhard von Rad, *Genesis: A Commentary* (London: SCM Press, 1961), p. 49.
3   Meric Srokosz and Rebecca S. Watson, *Blue Planet, Blue God: The Bible and the Sea* (London: SCM Press, 2017), p. 23.
4   Hermann Gunkel (trans. K.W. Whitney), *Creation and Chaos in the Primeval era and the Eschaton: A Religio-Historical Study of Genesis 1 and Revelation 12* (Grand Rapids MI: Eerdmans, 2006), pp. 78-111.
5   Isaac Asimov, *In the Beginning* (London: New English Library, 1981), p. 19.
6   John Day, *God's Conflict with the Dragon and the Sea: Echoes of a Canaanite Myth in the Old Testament* (Cambridge: Cambridge University Press, 1985).
7   Margaret Baker, *Temple Theology: An Introduction* (London: SPCK, 2004), p. 62.

2

Beside the Syrian Sea

In simple trust like theirs who heard
beside the Syrian sea
the gracious calling of the Lord,
let us, like them, without a word
rise up and follow thee.

John Greenleaf Whittier

The hymn 'Dear Lord and Father of Mankind' has curious origins. Its words are taken from the poem 'The Brewing of Soma' by the nineteenth-century American Quaker John Greenleaf Whittier. The full version of the poem contrasts the ancient Vedic Hindu ritual of using a hallucinogenic drink to stir up religious feelings with the Quaker practice of waiting in silence to hear God's 'still, small voice'. Whittier juxtaposes the drug-fuelled ritual that takes place on the banks of the Gihon (a river mentioned in Genesis and later thought to flow through the Hindu Kush) with the wordless response of the fishermen Simon, Andrew, James, and John to Jesus' call to follow him 'beside the Syrian sea' – the Sea of Galilee. According to the gospels, many of the key events in Jesus' ministry took place on or by the Sea of Galilee. As well as being where he called his first disciples, it is here that Jesus taught the crowds, healed the sick, calmed the storm, walked on water, and where, after rising from the dead, he appeared to his disciples. It is as if the Sea of Galilee has special spiritual significance.

Just as poets often draw on landscapes to express moods and feelings, so, too, do the gospel writers make dramatic use of 'place'. It is in the harsh, barren, desert wilderness that Jesus' vocation is tested and confirmed: it is where he is tempted by Satan, facing his inner demons, and it is where he is baptised by John, and so aligns himself with John's ministry of repentance. From there, the gospels take us to the more hospitable, rural territory of

Galilee. It is here that Jesus' ministry develops and flourishes, and where his disciples begin to grasp the reality of who he is. It is then in the city of Jerusalem that Jesus confronts earthly power, his true identity is denied, his followers desert him, and he is executed. Following his resurrection, Jesus returns to rural Galilee, where he charges his disciples to 'make disciples of all the nations' (Matthew 28:19).

These different types of place – the wilderness, the rural backwater of Galilee, and the busy city of Jerusalem – are associated with different gospel stories and evoke different thoughts and ideas: the wilderness with testing and discovery, the rural with growth and flourishing, and the city with power and conflict. As Philip Sheldrake says of landscapes, they 'are more than physical features. They are the geography of our imagination', having 'a capacity to carry us beyond ourselves' and induce 'our first intimations of the sacred.'[1] It is hard to read the gospels and not sense something special about Galilee. For Christians, Galilee is 'the sphere of revelation and redemption', to quote John Inge.[2]

There is no more evocative biblical story of 'place' than the account at the end of John's gospel of the risen Christ's encounter with his disciples on the shore of the Sea of Galilee. It is here that miracles, reconciliation, and spiritual transformation take place, told in a way loaded with hidden, symbolic meaning. The disciples, having returned to fishing, have spent the night without catching anything, when the risen Christ, standing on the beach, says to them:

> 'Children, you have no fish, have you?' They answered him, 'No.' He said to them, 'Cast the net to the right side of the boat, and you will find some.' So they cast it, and now they were not able to haul it in because there were so many fish. That disciple whom Jesus loved said to Peter, 'It is the Lord!' When Simon Peter heard that it was the Lord, he put on some clothes, for he was naked, and jumped into the lake. But the other disciples came in the boat, dragging the net full of fish, for they were not far from the land, only about a hundred yards off.
>
> (John 21:5-8)

After the miraculous haul of fish (and its allusion to the disciples being called to be 'fishers of people'), the gospel goes on to describe Jesus having a breakfast with the disciples of bread and fish (21:9-14) (echoing the last supper and the feeding of the five thousand), and his conversation with Simon Peter, when he asks the disciple three times if he loves him (as if to free him from the guilt of denying knowing his friend three times before the cock crowed when Jesus was arrested) (21:15-17). The gospel ends with Jesus telling Simon Peter and 'the disciple whom Jesus loved' to 'Follow me' (21:22).

The end of John's gospel is both resolving and mysterious, as if to bring its account of Jesus to a conclusion yet simultaneously stir up powerful ideas and images to reflect on. Consciously or unconsciously, there is a striking similarity in mood between the end of John's gospel and the final scene of *The Tempest*, the more spiritual of Shakespeare's plays. Here, too, it is on a beach where events are miraculously resolved and relationships restored, orchestrated by the mystical presence of Prospero. The play ends leaving the audience pondering who this mysterious person really is. The beach is a fitting location for the ending of both the gospel and the play. Sometimes described as a 'liminal' space, the seashore is where the interaction of land and water – solid and liquid – speaks of the closeness of two realms or states of being: the physical and the spiritual. For Christians familiar with John's gospel, it is hard to stand on a beach and not be influenced consciously or subconsciously by the story of the risen Christ's encounter with his disciples. It is these sort of ideas and connections that create a sense of 'place'.

In their various ways, all the gospels portray the shore of the Sea of Galilee as a border between the physical and spiritual realms, where Earth and Heaven meet. It is perhaps for this reason that Jesus appears equally at home on water or land. He sleeps through the storm and is unperturbed when he awakes, while the disciples – many of them fisherman – are terrified by the storm (Matthew 8:23-27, Mark 4:35-41 and Luke 8:22-25). He walks on water as if on solid ground (Mark 6:45-52, John 6:15-21), while Peter nearly drowns when he tries to follow him (Matthew 14:22-33).

The Sea of Galilee is such a familiar biblical name that it can come as a surprise to discover that it is probably a misnomer. Thirteen miles long and eight miles across at its widest point, this 'sea' is in fact an inland freshwater lake, and there are no references in ancient texts other than the gospels to it being called the Sea of Galilee. According to the first-century Romano-Jewish historian Josephus and his contemporary, the Roman natural philosopher Pliny the Elder, this expanse of water was known as the Lake of Gennesaret, Tiberias, or Tarichaeae. In contrast, both Mark and Matthew's gospels refer only to the Sea of Galilee, while John's gospel uses both Sea of Galilee and Sea of Tiberias. It is only Luke's gospel that mentions the lake of Gennesaret, with Luke reserving the use of the word 'sea' to refer to the Mediterranean, which features prominently in the gospel's companion volume, the Acts of the Apostles. The absence of references to the Sea of Galilee in non-biblical literature, as well as variations on its name, may simply reflect different local

practice – just as the English Channel is known as *La Manche* ('The Sleeve')
in France. However, it also raises the intriguing possibility that the use of
the word 'sea' has a deliberate theological purpose. One possibility is that it
was introduced by early Christians to show Jesus as the fulfilment of Isaiah's
prophecy, when:

> there will be no gloom for those who were in anguish. In the former
> time he brought into contempt the land of Zebulun and the land of
> Naphtali, but in the latter time he will make glorious the way of the sea,
> the land beyond the Jordan, Galilee of the nations.
>
> (Isaiah 9:1)

This passage is quoted in Matthew's gospel when Jesus begins his ministry
(4:12-17), and some scholars suggest that by calling the lake the Sea of Galilee
the gospel writer may be seeking to connect Jesus with Isaiah's prophecy, as
if to emphasise the glory of what Jesus did on or near the lake, 'the way of
the sea'.

There is, however, another possible explanation. Surrounded by high hills,
the Sea of Galilee is prone to rushing winds and sudden storms that, although
not as severe as those experienced at sea, are nevertheless sufficiently violent
to cause terror. It is on this 'sea' that Jesus is shown to be the Messiah or
saviour. As Matthew's gospel puts it:

> And when he got into the boat, his disciples followed him. A windstorm
> arose on the sea, so great the boat was being swamped by waves; but he
> was asleep. And they went and woke him up, saying, 'Lord, save us! We
> are perishing!' And he said to them, 'Why are you afraid, you of little
> faith?' Then he got up and rebuked the winds and the sea; and there
> was a dead calm. They were amazed, saying, 'What sort of a man is this,
> that even the winds and the sea obey him?'
>
> (Matthew 8:23-27)

Later in the gospel, Jesus is able to walk on the surface of the water:

> Immediately he made the disciples get into the boat and go on ahead
> to the other side, while he dismissed the crowds. And after he had
> dismissed the crowds, he went up the mountain by himself to pray.
> When evening came, he was there alone, but by this time the boat,
> battered by the waves, was far from the land, for the wind was against
> them. And early in the morning he came walking towards them on
> the lake. But when the disciples saw him walking on the lake, they

were terrified, saying, 'It is a ghost!' And they cried out in fear. But immediately Jesus spoke to them and said, 'Take heart, it is I; do not be afraid.'

Peter answered him, 'Lord, if it is you, command me to come to you on the water.' He said, 'Come.' So Peter got out of the boat, started walking on the water, and came towards Jesus. But when he noticed the strong wind, he became frightened, and beginning to sink, he cried out, 'Lord, save me!' Jesus immediately reached out his hand and caught him, saying to him, 'You of little faith, why did you doubt?' When they got into the boat, the wind ceased. And those in the boat worshipped him, saying, 'Truly you are the Son of God.'

(Matthew 14:22-33)

In these two, related, stories there are strong allusions to the divine action in creation in Genesis: control over chaotic water, and movement over its surface. It is as if Matthew uses powerful imagery to show a new dimension to God's saving work: that Jesus is acting with divine power and has control over the most powerful biblical symbol of chaos and evil. Peter, who is representative of all who struggle with their faith, has no such power, but is nevertheless saved by Jesus' intervention. When Jesus stills the storm, the disciples ask, 'What sort of a man is this, that even the winds and the sea obey him?' When Jesus walks on water, the disciples answer their own question: 'Truly you are the Son of God.'

Whether or not it was a deliberate intention of the gospel-writers to use the word 'sea' instead of lake to heighten the dramatic effect of their gospels, it certainly does so. It would, of course, have been absurd to call the Sea of Galilee an 'ocean' – the true image of chaos – but the transition from lake to sea adds to the sense of Jesus' ministry taking place on a borderland, and of divine power in his actions.

There is an echo of Jesus stilling the storm and walking on water in the gripping account of Paul's final voyage in the Acts of the Apostles. The background to this dramatic episode is that Paul was under arrest, on the charge of blasphemy, and was being transported to stand trial in Rome (he was a Roman citizen). The way that Luke portrays Paul in this story is not as someone deprived of his liberty but as a courageous apostle guided by God. Although Paul was a prisoner, travelling under Roman orders, he is shown as believing it was God's will that he should make the journey to Rome, as this would give him the opportunity to proclaim Christ in the heart of the Roman Empire. We are told that the voyage took place at the end of the Mediterranean sailing season, when the danger of sea travel was increasing. Rather than remain in Crete over the winter, it was decided to risk sailing to Italy. It was on this final leg of the voyage that the ship encountered two weeks of stormy weather, culminating in Paul and all others on board being shipwrecked on the island of Malta. The dramatic account in Acts reads like an adventure story with Paul its hero: by his prayer and initiative 'all were brought safely to land' (27:44). As the sequel to Luke's gospel, the Acts of the Apostles show how the apostles – especially Paul – echo Jesus in their ministry. As Tom Wright points out, for example, the climactic end to Acts parallels the trial and crucifixion of Jesus at the end of Luke's gospel, portraying Paul as a disciple who is prepared to follow Jesus 'on the way of the cross'.[3]

For Paul, 'the way of the cross' involved danger at sea and being shipwrecked. This comes across in the parallels between the account of Paul's stormy sea voyage and Luke's version of the story of Jesus stilling the storm on the lake. In Luke's gospel, Jesus calmly says to the terrified disciples after they woke him up during the storm, 'Where is your faith?', after which he commands the storm to cease (Luke 8:22-25). While Paul does not carry out such a miracle he is, nevertheless, similarly portrayed as calm and collected while all around him are terrified. Paul, the prisoner, who had already been shipwrecked three times and spent a day and night adrift at sea (2 Corinthians 11:25), is portrayed as taking control of the situation, advising expert sailors – just as Jesus, the carpenter, took control during the storm, advising expert fishermen. After receiving a divine revelation that all would be safe, Paul addresses those in command of the ship, telling them, 'So keep up your courage, for I have faith in God that it will be as I have been told' (Acts 27:25).

The parallel between Jesus and Paul extends further. After stilling the storm and disembarking from the boat, Jesus performs two miracles: casting out demons from the Gadarene demoniac and healing the daughter of Jairus. After reaching land, Paul is apparently miraculously saved after a snake gripped onto his hand, and then he went to cure the father of Publius, 'the leading man of the island', who was sick with fever and dysentery. If, in the gospels, Peter symbolises Jesus' followers who stumble along in their discipleship, learning from their mistakes, Paul in the Acts of the Apostles speaks of a different sort of discipleship: of one whose conversion on the road to Damascus gave him clarity of his convictions. The contrast is made against the backdrop of the 'sea'.

The sea also plays an important symbolic role in the final book of the Bible, the Revelation of St John the Divine. Revelation is an extraordinary piece of literature. Written by John while he was imprisoned on the Greek island of Patmos, probably under the persecution of Christians by the Roman emperor Domitian, Revelation is steeped in surreal, mysterious imagery, much of it relating to the sea. The imagery is so strange that it has even been suggested that John wrote Revelation under the influence of eating the hallucinogenic mushrooms found in the Greek islands. More likely, though, is that John draws on, and reworks, apocalyptic visions from the Book of Daniel, the prophecy of Ezekiel, and the symbolism of the First Temple, in order to convey a hidden message that would be understood only by those familiar with these sources.

Revelation contains a coded theological attack on the Roman Empire. Rome is not mentioned directly, but is referred to throughout Revelation as 'Babylon' – making the connection with a previous imperial power that caused devastation to Israel, including the destruction of the First Temple following the siege of Jerusalem in 589 BCE. Revelation also draws on the oracle against Tyre in the prophecy of Ezekiel. Tyre had been a major Phoenician port on the coast of what is now Lebanon, and part of the greatest maritime and commercial power in ancient times. The abuse of the Phoenicians' economic power, generated by sea trade, led Ezekiel to prophecy Tyre's destruction:

> Because your heart is proud
> and you have said, 'I am a god;
> I sit in the seat of the gods,
> in the heart of the seas',
> yet you are but a mortal, and no god,
> though you compare your mind
> with the mind of a god.
> (Ezekiel 28:2)

Shortly after Ezekiel's prophecy Tyre was besieged by the Babylonian king Nebuchadnezzar, and two centuries later the city was destroyed by Alexander the Great. By using coded language to liken the great maritime and economic power of Rome to Tyre, Revelation's hidden message would have been clear to those who could see beyond the symbolism – but presumably not to those holding John captive.

Revelation contains much sea imagery. Some of it relates to the First Temple in Jerusalem, constructed, as we have seen, to be a microcosm of the cosmos as understood by the ancient Israelites. For instance, the 'sea of glass, mixed with fire' (15:2) is probably a reference to a symbolic physical representation of the sea in the temple, which was constructed to represent the creation story in the opening verses of Genesis. Another, more oblique, sea allusion is the 'song of Moses, the servant of God and the song of the Lamb' (15:3-4) which begins 'Great and amazing are your deeds, / Lord God the Almighty!' This is most likely a reference to the 'Song of the Sea' in Exodus, which follows the story of the crossing of the Red Sea, and begins, 'I will sing to the Lord for he has triumphed gloriously; / horse and rider he has thrown into the sea.' (15:1). What John appears to do in this section of his Revelation is draw a parallel between passing through the waters of baptism and passing through the Red Sea. In Christ, the journey to salvation involves passing through these baptismal waters, just as for the Israelites it involved a journey through the Red Sea.

The most curious – and most significant – reference to the sea in Revelation, however, occurs in chapter 21, verse 1: 'Then I saw a new heaven and new earth; for the first heaven and the first earth had passed away, and the sea was no more.' This is John's apocalyptic vision of what will be when God re-creates the cosmos. The prophecy of Isaiah also includes an image of the perfected age to come where all creatures will live in harmony at a time when 'the earth will be full of the knowledge of the Lord / as the waters cover the sea' (Isaiah 11:9). In contrast, the new creation in Revelation is not like Isaiah's 'peaceable kingdom' and is no longer a rural idyll like the Garden of Eden, it is a city – the new Jerusalem – although with an allusion to Eden, it does contain a garden and has a river flowing through it. But more striking still in Revelation is the image of the re-ordering of the cosmos – Heaven and Earth are renewed, and in the process 'the sea was no more.'

The absence of the sea in John's vision may at first seem strange, but it is totally consistent with the portrayal of the sea elsewhere in Revelation. In chapter 13, the terrifying beast, which wreaks destruction on the world, rises out of the sea. Then, in chapter 20, on the Day of Judgment it is the sea, as well as Death and Hades, which will give up its dead to stand before God. The sea, then, in Revelation is associated with evil and death. This harks back to the idea of the sea being a remnant of the chaotic primordial state. In John's vision of the new creation, though, the waters of chaos above and below the firmament vanish. What God removes is twofold: first, the presence of chaos, which is associated with evil and death; and second, the means by which God's judgement was previously executed on humanity. After the Flood, and the saving work of Moses, God put aside his 'bow of war'. When salvation through Christ – the second Moses – is complete, and the final judgment has taken place, a new, perfected, creation will exist in which God has removed the most destructive weapon of all – the waters of the deep.

Behind the numerous biblical references to the sea, lakes, and rivers lay the ideas set out in the opening passages of Genesis: that these are created by God out of the primordial waters of chaos – the deep – of which the oceans are the remnant. In the background – and in the case of the Flood, the foreground – is the threat of a return to pre-creation chaos, until creation is perfected and 'the sea was no more'. This world-view clearly owed much to the development of Judaism on the eastern edge of the Mediterranean, and to the experience of mariners who plied their trade in its relatively calm, tide-less and land-bound waters but knew of the wild, tidal, open Atlantic that lay beyond to the west.

Early Christianity inherited this understanding of the sea from its Jewish roots, and this is felt in the way the gospel writers present the stories of Jesus and the Sea of Galilee: only divine power can control its waters. However, as Christianity began to spread to maritime communities around the Mediterranean, alternative theological ideas about the sea began to interact with those underpinning the Bible. It is to these that we now turn.

1 Philip Sheldrake, *Spirituality and Theology: Christian Living and the Doctrine of God* (London: Darton, Longman and Todd, 1998) pp. 167-8.
2 John Inge, *A Christian Theology of Place* (Aldershot: Ashgate, 2003), p. 49.
3 Tom Wright, *Paul: A Biography* (London: SPCK, 2018), p. 376.

3

A Vast Sea of Mystery

Those who live by the sea can hardly form a single
thought of which the sea would not be part.
Hermann Broch, *The Spell*

Origen, who is widely regarded as the first significant Christian theologian, called the scriptures 'a vast sea of mystery'.[1] Like many influential early Christians, Origen was familiar with the sea. He came from the Egyptian coastal city of Alexandria and travelled by sea to Rome, Athens, and Palestine in his work as a Christian scholar. It is not hard to imagine Origen using his time on board ship to look out to sea and apply his mind, shaped by classical philosophy, to reflect on the meaning of the scriptures.

The spread of Christianity owes much to sea travel, not least in its formative period in the late-first and second centuries BCE. Many of the Christian communities mentioned in the New Testament were located in coastal towns and cities in the eastern Mediterranean or Aegean, so much so that this region is known as 'the cradle of Christianity'. The best documented traveller of the early Church is St Paul. Piecing together the journeys referred to in the Acts of the Apostles and the Pauline epistles it is estimated that Paul travelled about 10,000 miles, which included several sea voyages. We know, for instance, that he sailed to Salamis in Cyprus, to Perga in Pamphylia, to Antioch in Syria, and on several occasions back to Palestine. As we have already seen, his most famous voyage, described in Acts 27, was to Italy as a prisoner, when he was shipwrecked off Malta.

Since Paul was an experienced sea-traveller (and as a tent-maker, perhaps also a sail-maker), and because his journeys took him to many coastal communities, it is not surprising that he used sailing metaphors to describe the Christian faith. Several of these have been lost in translation, diminishing the sense of his engagement with seafaring communities. As David Williams points out, when Paul refers to the 'servants of Christ' who are 'stewards of God's mysteries' and called to live a life of service (1 Corinthians 4:1) he uses the Greek word for 'under-rowers' on board ship, whose duties would include the dirty work of cleaning out the bilge. Christian service involves a willingness to do the least desirable tasks for the sake of God's kingdom. Likewise, the quality of leadership Paul mentions in relation to using the gifts of the spirit (1 Corinthians 12:28) is the Greek word for helmsman-ship. The helmsman must be astute, understanding tides, currents, and winds in order to steer. So, too, the gift of Christian leadership involves working creatively with the spiritual gifts of others. Another instance of a change of meaning occurs in Paul's dispute with Peter over the Gentile mission. We are told that while Paul would eat with Gentiles, Peter 'drew back' from doing so, but a more accurate translation would be that Peter 'trimmed his sails' (Galatians 2:12).[2]

The decision to extend the Christian mission beyond Judaism to Gentiles, and the subsequent contact between Jewish and non-Jewish Christians, had a profound effect on the development of Christianity. One important consequence was that it led to an interaction between Jewish theology and Greek philosophy. As early Christian theologians such as Origen sought to make sense of the Christian story, they did so not only by referring to the Hebrew scriptures, of which they understood Jesus Christ to be the fulfilment, but also to the classical philosophy with which they were familiar. The synergy of religious thought rooted in Judaism and classical philosophy gave an important shape to Christian theology of the Patristic period, the era of the Church Fathers whose theological influence continues to this day. If, for Joseph Conrad, the Mediterranean was the 'nursery' of sailors,[3] for the early Church it was also the nursery of theologians. In coastal towns and cities around the Mediterranean and Aegean many of the great thinkers of the early Church sought to deepen their understanding of the Christian faith by seeing it through the lens of the classical philosophers. Plato, in particular, was an important influence, and regarded by many as pre-figuring Christianity in his work.

A key figure in bringing Neo-Platonism into Christian theology was Justin Martyr. Born of Greek parents early in the second century, Justin, like his near contemporary Origen, was steeped in classical philosophy. It was while meditating in solitude on the seashore at Ephesus that Justin met an elderly man who disputed with him over the Platonic doctrine of the soul and told him of Jewish prophecy and of Jesus Christ as the fulfilment of that prophecy. It was following this encounter by the sea, with someone probably only a generation away from the Christian community known to Paul, that Justin converted to Christianity. Rather than reject classical philosophy, Justin sought to integrate it with his new-found faith, seeing a parallel between God as revealed in Jewish and Christian scriptures and Plato's understanding of the transcendent God beyond human comprehension. He saw as well a direct connection between the Platonic concept of the *logos* – the transcendent divine mind that gives order and meaning to the cosmos – and the Christian understanding of Jesus Christ as *logos* – the Word made flesh – from the opening of John's gospel. Justin's conversion by the sea and subsequent work as a theologian helped shaped the course of Christianity, as Neo-Platonism (not without controversy) gained influence.

The interaction between Jewish and non-Jewish Christians took place at another level as well. As Christianity shifted away from its Jewish roots it absorbed the cultural practices and insights of other communities, picking up Greek, Roman, North African, and other influences along the way. Both the intellectual and social influences of Mediterranean cultures on Christianity are evident from references made to the sea in the early Church. If, as Bernard McGinn suggests, the Jews of antiquity were the 'landlubbers from the Mediterranean littoral',[4] then many gentile Christians came from confident seafaring communities that had a more positive outlook on the sea. As Lenček and Bosker point out in their history of beaches, the sea was 'as much a playground as workplace' for classical Greeks and Romans.[5] It was among such people that Christianity first took hold, and as a result a different attitude towards the sea – or at least towards the Mediterranean and Aegean – began to influence Christian thinkers and leaders.

We can see this change of tack in, for example, the writings of Gregory of Nazianzus. Gregory lived in the fourth century and was the son of the Bishop of Nazianzus, a city in the inland region of Cappadocia in what is now Turkey. Gregory later succeeded his father as bishop before becoming Archbishop of Constantinople (now Istanbul), and was part of an influential circle of theologians known as the Cappadocian Fathers who helped eliminate Arianism (which denied the divinity of Christ) as a major force within the Church. In a comment that resonates with Joseph Conrad's observation of our love-hate relationship with the sea, Gregory observed that, 'The sea ruins one man, while another spreads his shining sails and as he passes over the water looks down smiling at this great grave of the shipwrecked.'[6] Gregory wrote with great personal feeling. As a young man he was shipwrecked on a voyage between Rhodes and Alexandria, while as Archbishop of Constantinople he was based at a major port on the inland sea, Propontis (or Sea of Marmara) that linked the Aegean and Black Sea. Gregory was typical of Christian leaders of the time: familiar with living by the sea, experienced in sea travel and its dangers, and greatly aware that the Christian mission depended as much upon sailors as it did upon the missionaries who sailed with them. No wonder he had such mixed feelings.

One of the most eloquent figures in early Christian history was Gregory's successor but one as Archbishop of Constantinople, St John Chrysostom. Chrysostom means 'golden tongued', and John, who lived from *c.*350 until 407, was given this name for his gifts as a preacher and public speaker. We can get a hint of his oratorical skills from his many surviving sermons and other writings, a striking feature of which is the frequent use of sea imagery. John's fascination with the sea is evident in the third of his *Eight Sermons on the Book of Genesis*. Here he echoes Origen by using the vastness of the ocean as a metaphor for the breadth of what can be found in the scriptures, although:

> In the ocean of the Scriptures there is no buffeting from waves: this ocean is calmer than any harbour, there is no need to descend into the gloomy caverns of the deep, nor commit the safety of one's person to the rush of irrational waters. Instead, here there is a strong light brighter than the sun's rays, there is deep peace, no tempest in the offing, the value of which is found so great as to defy description.[7]

John came from Antioch (now Antakya), which is on the river Orontes and not far from the coast, so it is possible that he would have been familiar with the sea and ships from a young age. However, as archbishop in the maritime environment of Constantinople, it is not surprising that John developed a fascination for the sea or used its imagery to communicate his thinking on religion. The latter part of John's life was dominated by theological disputes, to the extent that he was exiled and imprisoned, finally in Pitsunda on the eastern shore of the Black Sea, where he died. During his exile, John received help from Olympias, an elderly deaconess from Constantinople, with whom he kept up a pastoral correspondence. Nearing death, when Olympias was also facing difficult times, John drew upon his experiences of a terrible voyage to offer hope to his friend:

> Come now, let me soften the wound of your sadness, and disperse the sad cogitations which compose this gloomy cloud of care. What is it which upsets your mind, and occasions your grief and despondency? Is it the fierce and lowering storm which has overtaken the Churches and enveloped all with the darkness of a moonless night, which is

growing to a head every day, and has already wrought many lamentable shipwrecks? ... We behold a sea heaved up from its lowest depths, some sailors floating dead, others struggling in the waves, the planks of the vessel breaking up, the masts sprung, the canvas torn, the oars dashed out of the sailors' hands, the pilots, seated on the deck, clasping their knees with their hands, and crying aloud at the hopelessness of their situation; neither sky nor sea clearly visible, but all one impenetrable gloom, and monsters of the deep attacking the shipwrecked crew on every side ... Yet, when I see all this, I do not despair, when I consider who is the Disposer of this whole universe — One who masters the storm, not by the contrivance of art, but can calm it by His nod alone.... Let none of these things which happen vex you ... but continually beseech Jesus Christ, whom you serve ... and all these troubles will be dissolved; if not in an instant of time, that is because He is waiting till wickedness has grown to a height, and then he will suddenly change the storm into a calm.[8]

John's language demonstrates the power of sea imagery. Anyone who has experienced a bad storm at sea would know of the feelings such language evokes, and of how much hope and trust is placed on someone likened to a pilot, whose skill in a dangerous situation saves lives.

The literary images of Christ as a pilot and troubled times as a storm at sea are matched by some of the most ancient Christian visual images. The oldest recorded image for Christ (which can commonly be seen today on car bumpers) is that of a fish. This is not so much a sea image as a pun from an acrostic, as the first letters from the Greek phrase 'Jesus Christ / Son of God / the Saviour' (*Iēsous Christos, Theou Yious Sōtēr*) form the Greek word for fish, *ichthys*. It is a highly appropriate symbol, as the fish conjures up images of Jesus' ministry by the Sea of Galilee: the call of fishermen to be disciples, the multiplication of the loaves and fishes, the miraculous catch of fish, and the meal of the resurrected Christ on the lake's shore. Another sea image from the early period of Christianity is the symbol of a cross as the crosspiece of a ship's anchor, with fish either side. This image is inscribed on the funerary slab of Priscilla in the Roman catacombs and thought to date from the third or fourth century. Here the cross is portrayed, like an anchor, as a source of spiritual stability in a world sufficiently turbulent to make Roman Christians literally go underground.

A third early Christian image is that of the ship. During the years of Christian persecution and ostracism this is an understandable symbol, drawing on the image of the ark and the Flood, and making the point that in a dangerous, hostile world the 'ship of the Church' offered spiritual security. St Ambrose, Bishop of Milan in the late fourth century, famously compared the Church to a ship and the cross to a ship's mast, and the symbol of the 'ship of the Church' became widespread. A good ship was required, because Ambrose regarded the sea with considerable mistrust. This is evident in the response he gave to the charge that by encouraging virginity he was threatening to depopulate the Roman Empire. It was war and the sea, not virginity, he said, that destroyed the human race. Ambrose's attitude may well have been influenced by the experience of his brother Satyrus, who survived being shipwrecked in a voyage to North Africa.

Ambrose's contemporary, St Augustine of Hippo, also made significant use of sea imagery. This is not surprising, as both his home city of Carthage and Hippo, of which he became bishop, were major ports on the North African coast. He, too, knew the waters between North Africa and Italy as he crossed them travelling to Rome, where he met Ambrose, whose influence was to change his life. Augustine's earliest extant work, *De Beata Vita*, an essay on what makes for 'the happy life', could hardly be more loaded with sea imagery, as it is an extended metaphor of life as a journey at sea during a storm. The way we approach life, Augustine argues, is like the attitude of different sailors: those who make little effort and stay close to the shore; those that venture far out to sea, forgetting their homeland and often getting into danger; and those somewhere in-between, who are somewhat adventurous but who return to their home.

If Augustine drew upon his familiarity with the sea in writing this essay, more importantly, he drew further upon his own experiences of searching for meaning and spiritual fulfilment. Augustine's journey of faith was a troubled one, in which he rejected the Christianity of his childhood and turned first to Manicheism and then to the religion of the Greek philosophers, especially Plato, before rediscovering Christianity (like his third category of sailor). For Augustine, the discovery of the happiness came from getting his bearings and navigating his life by Christ, 'the North Star'. This discovery was, for Augustine, the culmination of a challenging intellectual journey, which is why *De Beata Vita* begins:

> Great and noble Theodore, if to reach the port of philosophy from which, indeed, a person can proceed to the region and field of a happy life, the course must be founded upon rational thought and individual will, I know not whether I would be speaking carelessly in saying that

few men have reached this port, since at present, only a rare few attain it.[9]

From his understanding of Greek philosophy, Augustine was clearly familiar with Homer's *Odyssey*. This is evident in *De Beata Vita* when he refers to the Sirens, the mysterious birdlike women who, in the *Odyssey*, use enchanting music to lure sailors to their death on the rocky coastline. Augustine's quote is evidence of one of the intriguing consequences of the interaction between Christianity and other Mediterranean cultures, which is the Christianisation of non-Christian festivals, rituals and texts. The most notable instance of the latter, through the influence of Neo-Platonism, is the *Odyssey*. This has been studied in depth by Hugo Rahner who has demonstrated how the story was used as a Christianised myth and as an allegory of the Christian life.[10] As well as being perhaps the greatest work of classical mythology, the *Odyssey* is also one of the greatest works about the sea. Set in the Mediterranean, it tells of Odysseus' long journey from the Trojan wars to return to his wife, Penelope, and his home in Ithaca. The journey is fraught with dangers and temptations, with the sea playing a pivotal role. Odysseus faces setback after setback until eventually, after twenty years, he reaches his destination.

The *Odyssey* is full of wonderful sea imagery as well as a host of strange and often hostile places and creatures. After Odysseus begins his voyage home his ships are driven by wind to land at Ismarus, where he and his crew fight the native Ciconians. As their journey continues they are driven off-course to the land of the Lotus-Eaters, where the taste of lotus removes the desire for some of the crew to return home. Those that remain sail to the land of the Cyclops, where they fight the one-eyed giant Polyphemus. Next, on the island of Aeolia, Aeolus, who guards the winds, gives Odysseus a leather bag containing the boisterous winds, but when his crew open the bag they are driven backwards on their voyage, landing in the country of man-eating giants called Laestrygonians. Sailing to Aeaea they encounter the enchantress Circe. Odysseus makes love to her, and she sends him to visit Hades, the underworld, beyond the Pillars of Hercules (i.e. the Atlantic Ocean) before he can continue his journey home. They next encounter the Sirens before passing the whirlpool Charybdis and the six-headed monster Scylla, both of which kill many of the crew. Those that remain next encounter a storm sent by the god Zeus that only Odysseus survives, and he narrowly escapes death when his raft is sucked into Charybdis. Odysseus is washed up on the island of Ogygia where the goddess Calypso keeps him as her lover for seven years. Eventually the gods release him, but before he can complete his journey,

Poseidon, god of the Sea, causes a storm that destroys his raft. Odysseus is saved by the sea-goddess Leucothea, and eventually Phoenicians provide him with a ship on which he completes his voyage home.

At first sight such a story does not seem ripe for Christian interpretation. Yet Clement of Alexandria (*c.*150 to *c.*215) and Methodius of Olympus (died *c.*311) were almost alone among early Christian theologians in condemning the story. They regarded Odysseus' journey as being driven by earthly desires, and so he was unfit as a Christian role model. As Clement remarked, 'Men attach themselves to this world as certain kinds of seaweed cling to the rocks by the seashore'.[11] Others treated the story very differently. The Cappadocian Father St Basil regarded the *Odyssey* as 'a hymn to virtue',[12] while St Jerome spoke of the need to 'turn deaf ears to the death-bringing songs of the Sirens as we pass them on our way', and Tertullian described Homer as a 'prince of poets'.[13] Like Plato, Homer was regarded by some as a Christian theologian before his time whose work prefigured Jesus Christ (although many scholars now believe that Homer was not an individual, but a group of writers who collectively wrote the *Odyssey* and the other Homeric epic poem, the *Iliad*).

Three aspects of the *Odyssey* in particular captured the imagination of theologians. The voyage, with the ever-present threat of death from the sea, was seen in Christian terms as an allegory for the journey of the earthly life and the final destination of Heaven. Being a Christian and living with the threat of persecution or ostracism required the perseverance of Odysseus as he faced so many setbacks. The seductive Sirens, whose song lured sailors to their death, became a symbol for the deadly lust for earthly things that could undermine the Christian life and bring spiritual destruction, while the image of Odysseus lashed to the mast of his ship to enable him to sail past the Sirens (while his crew blocked their ears with wax) provided a graphic image of 'taking up the cross' to follow Christ. Odysseus, then, became an unlikely Christian hero whose determination was seen as demonstrating a quality required for Christian discipleship. Remarkably, the influence of the *Odyssey* in Christian thought lasted for centuries.

As well as influencing theology, the sea also played its part in the spiritual life of the early Church. Given the dangers of life at sea, it is not surprising that as the cult of the saints developed some became associated with the sea and seafaring and targeted for intercessory prayer. By far the most famous is St Nicholas. Little is known for sure of this saint beyond that he was Bishop of Myra in the province of Lycia in what is now Turkey sometime in the fourth century. Hagiography of Nicholas dates from about 500 years after his death, the first account of his life being written by St Methodius, Patriarch of

Constantinople, in the ninth century. What is clear is that Nicholas gained a reputation as a miracle worker so that by the sixth century a cult had developed around him. 'May St Nicholas hold the tiller' became a common phrase to wish sailors well in the Aegean and Ionian seas, and Nicholas became patron saint of sailors in the East, with many coastal churches and chapels in this region (and elsewhere) dedicated to him.

One legend, set to song in Benjamin Britten's cantata *St Nicholas*, is that Nicholas was on board a ship during a storm and, in a Christ-like way, stilled the storm by prayer. Another is that the sailors on board a ship in distress in the eastern Mediterranean, knowing the bishop's reputation, cried out to him, even though he was many miles away. Soon a strange figure miraculously appeared on board and helped the crew push the grounded ship away before it was dashed on the rocks. The figure then vanished. The relieved sailors sought a safe harbour, and then went to a church to give thanks to God for being saved. They arrived in Myra, and the church they chose was the cathedral where, to their amazement, they met the mysterious person who had appeared on board – it was bishop Nicholas. When asked how he heard their cries for help and how he came to their rescue, Nicholas is said to have replied that a life devoted to God allows someone to be so clear-sighted as to see the needs of others, and so aware of their needs as to respond to them.

Other saints, too, are associated with safety at sea because of their real or legendary exploits. These include St Erasmus of Formia, also known as St Elmo, who is reputed to have continued preaching after nearly being struck by lightning. For this reason, the electrical discharge that can occur on a ship's mast during a storm became known as 'St Elmo's fire', and a sign of the saint's protection. Prayers to such saints straddle religious devotion and superstition, things that often go hand in hand among sailors.

Bernard McGinn has argued that as well as influencing popular devotion and public prayer, the sea – or more specifically the ocean – provided a powerful symbol alongside the desert in the early development of Christian mysticism. This branch of Christian spirituality owes much to Neo-Platonism, drawing on the Platonic objective of being in union with God. Plato used the image of the vastness of the sea to express the goal of mysticism, which he described as 'turning towards the great sea of the beautiful.'[14] Christian ascetics were attracted to this image, living their lives with the purpose of achieving 'mystical union' with God. The first reference to the ocean in Christian mystical writing is by Evagrius Ponticus in the fourth century. Evagrius was a scholar who lived for a time in Constantinople and was a trusted friend of, amongst others, St Basil and Gregory of Nazianzus. After leaving Constantinople, he eventually became an ascetic living in the Egyptian desert, where his scholarship became focused on monasticism. Evagrius wrote about the spiritual goal of mystical union: the sense of being 'at one with', or 'absorbed into', God. Evagrius described salvation through Christ in terms of being reunited with God using the image of rivers flowing back to the sea to represent regaining lost unity with the divine. The power of this image stems from the mingling of waters which become indistinguishable. This imagery was taken up centuries later by the American poet Emily Dickinson, who is perhaps the most spiritual of the great sea-poets, in her poem 'My River Runs to Thee' which, rather like the Song of Songs, speaks of God in erotic terms:

> My river runs to thee –
> Blue Sea! Wilt welcome me?
> My river waits reply –
> Oh Sea – look graciously –
> I'll fetch thee Brooks
> From spotted nooks –
> *Say* – Sea – Take *Me*!

Sea imagery of this kind is also found in the writings of Evagrius' pupil John Cassian, and fellow Neo-Platonists John Scotus Eriugena (the ninth-century Irish theologian who described the divine nature in terms of 'the sea of infinite goodness ready to give itself to those wishing to participate in it'), Meister Eckhart (the thirteenth/fourteenth-century German who, quoting John of Damascus, described God as 'a sea of infinite substance, and consequently indistinct'), and later still Nicholas of Cusa. Nicholas, who was made a cardinal by Pope Nikolas V, is regarded as one of the most brilliant thinkers of the fifteenth century. His most influential work, *De docta ignorantia* (*Of Learned Ignorance*) deals with the problem of reconciling the finite and infinite, and Nicholas writes that his answer to the problem came as a divine revelation while sailing to Greece. As humans cannot grasp God's infinite nature by rational knowledge, Nicholas argues that the limits of rational enquiry need to be met by speculation that blurs the borders of rational knowledge and ignorance, thus causing what he termed a 'coincidence of opposites'. For Nicholas, like Augustine before him, his speculation leads to Christ who alone is able to bridge the finitude of humanity and the infinity of God, who 'As God … forgave sins, raised the dead, transformed nature, commanded spirits, the sea, and the winds. He walked on water and established a law in fullness of supply for all laws.'[15] What part did the sea play in Nicholas' moment of insight? Certainly, his thinking was influenced by

Augustine and Classical philosophers, who draw upon the sea as a metaphor. As Marjorie O'Rourke Boyle puts it, for Neo-Platonists the sea 'is the precise and perfect site for divine illumination'.[16]

⸻

If it is possible to make any general observations about Christian attitudes towards the sea between New Testament times and the centuries that followed, three stand out. First, there is a noticeable absence of references to the sea and chaos in patristic and later texts. There are several plausible reasons for this. As the Christian mission became focused on the Mediterranean and Aegean, the perils of the ocean were largely put aside. This was partly due to the experiences of those spreading the faith – they travelled by sea, and while they knew of its dangers (and some had first-hand experience), the sea was also familiar to them. It was something to be cautious, not fearful, of. Perhaps more significantly, from the late first century the expectation of the *parousia* – the end of the world, and Christ's second coming – began to fade. It was no longer regarded as imminent, but would take place in God's good time. Living the Christian life therefore became less focused on preparing for end times and more about ongoing discipleship. As a result, apocalyptic images – including that of the chaotic sea and its monsters – became less dominant in Christian thought.

The second, related, observation is that in the patristic period there was a greater emphasis on engagement with the sea. Again, there is perhaps both a pragmatic and a theological reason for this. Because the Christian mission relied so much on sea travel, it is unsurprising that this would feature in Christian writing. It is normal and natural for imagery from day-to-day life to permeate the literature of any culture, and bishops and theologians who lived in coastal communities and travelled by sea understandably found metaphors and allegories for the Christian life from what they were familiar with. However, in the years of Christian persecution and ostracism, there was also a growing emphasis on suffering being an important part of Christian discipleship. Christians are called to 'take up their cross'. Sea travel could be very uncomfortable and unpleasant through seasickness, and it could also be dangerous. It therefore became a way of taking up the cross. Shipwrecked bishops and missionaries no doubt regarded their experiences at sea as spiritual and integral to growing closer to the suffering Christ.

The third observation is the emerging importance of mysticism. No doubt humans have always found the sea mysteriously fascinating, and it is through the influence of classical philosophy that Christians discovered a way of relating this fascination to the ultimate mystery – God. These attitudes and ideas were honed by influential Christian thinkers and leaders who lived by and travelled in the relatively calm waters of the Mediterranean and Aegean. Soon, though, Christianity was to be taken beyond the Pillars of Hercules into the Atlantic and to the British Isles. As Christians began to engage with the primordial waters of chaos, a distinctive and significant form of spirituality emerged. It is to this that we now turn.

1   Jean Daniélou (trans. W. Mitchell), *Origen* (Eugene: Wipf and Stock, 1955), p. 173.
2   David J. Williams, *Paul's Metaphors: Their Context and Character* (Peabody, Mass: Hendrickson, 1999), pp. 195-7.
3   Joseph Conrad, *The Mirror of the Sea* (New York: Doubleday, Page & Co., 1924), p. 155.
4   Bernard McGinn, 'Ocean and Desert as Symbols of Mystical Absorption in the Christian Tradition', *Journal of Religion* 74 (1994), p. 156.
5   Lena Lenček and Gideon Bosker, *The Beach: The History of Paradise on Earth* (London: Pimlico, 1999), p. 26.
6   Hugo Rahner, *Greek Myths and Christian Mystery* (London: Burns and Oates, 1963), p. 344.
7   St John Chrysostom (trans. R.C. Hill), *Eight Sermons on the Book of Genesis* (Boston, MA: Holy Cross Orthodox Press, 2004), p. 53.
8   W.R.W. Stephens, *Saint John Chrysostom: His Life and Times*, 2nd edn. (London: John Murray, 1880), pp. 367-8.
9   St Augustine of Hippo (trans. L. Schopp), *The Happy Life* (London: B. Herder, 1939), p. 41.
10 Rahner, *Greek Myths*, pp. 328-86.
11 Ibid., p. 328.
12 Ibid., p. 332.
13 Ibid., p. 334.
14 McGinn, 'Ocean and Desert', pp. 157-8.
15 Nicholas of Cusa (trans. Jasper Hopkins), *Complete Philosophical and Theological Works of Nicholas of Cusa*, vol. 3 (Minneapolis: Arthur J Banning Press, 2001), p. 121.
16 Marjorie O'Rourke Boyle, 'Cusanus at Sea: The Topicality of Illuminative Discourse', *Journal of Religion*, 71 (1991), p. 184.

4

A Desert in the Ocean

The desert was created simply to be itself, not to be transformed by men into something else. So too the mountain and the sea.

Thomas Merton, *Thoughts in Solitude*

Sometime between 412 and 420 a monk, Eucherius, who later became Bishop of Lyons, wrote the following in a letter to Hilary, Bishop of Lérins: 'It was with great generosity that you once left your country and your relatives to penetrate the recesses of the desert as far as the Great Sea, but it is with greater virtue that you seek the desert a second time.'[1] The 'desert' Eucherius refers to is not a vast expanse of sand and rocky outcrops, but Lérins, a small group of islands in the 'Great Sea' of the Mediterranean off the south coast of France, near Cannes. Eucherius goes on to praise the spiritual virtues of solitude in the desert, which he calls 'a temple of God without walls', without any suggestion that he is not in the Egyptian desert from which he drew his inspiration. It is both an intriguing and revealing letter.

Eucherius was an early Western European convert to eastern-style desert monasticism. What his letter shows is the remarkable power this religious lifestyle could have in a very different setting. To an ascetic, the 'desert' may be found in any location where solitude can be experienced. This was – and is – often somewhere remote, but not necessarily the desert wilderness. In the eastern monastic tradition, for example, the forest became a favoured location for those drawn to the ascetic life. What is important is living out the fundamental principles of asceticism in any given location. The objective is an 'absorption into God', and this is aided by the removal of distractions and temptations – hence the emphasis on solitude. What is clear, though, is that the location can have a profound bearing on the experience. Much ascetic spiritual literature refers to the writer's physical surroundings. There is a strong sense that God is sought – and hopefully found – not only by an inner journey and the discipline of prayer, but by an interaction with the natural world.

The person most closely associated with taking the spiritual discipline of the Desert Fathers from the eastern Mediterranean to Western Europe is St Martin of Tours. Martin established the first monastery in Gaul in 361 with Hilary of Poitiers, and was a highly influential figure in Gaul and beyond. Eucherius was born during Martin's lifetime, and so was one of the first Western Europeans to be attracted to this newly emerging, and severely testing, form of religious life. Another key figure is John Cassian. A follower of the teachings of Origen, Cassian fled the desert of Scete in Egypt along with other Origenist monks following a theological dispute with Theophilus, Archbishop of Alexandria. Initially Cassian travelled to Constantinople to seek protection from the archbishop, John Chrysostom. Then, after going to Rome to appeal for help from Pope Innocent I, he accepted an invitation to establish a monastery on the south coast of Gaul, at Marseille. Here, at the Abbey of St Victor, Cassian developed close ties with the monks of Lérins.

The development of Christian monasticism in the eastern Mediterranean and its spread west not only coincided with the arrival of Christianity to the British Isles, but also had a considerable influence upon it. Long before Augustine arrived by sea to the Isle of Thanet in 597 to conduct a Christian mission on the instruction of Pope Gregory, Christianity had been brought by sea to the British Isles by an earlier phase of missionary activity along the established trade routes of the western seaboard. For centuries, sailors ventured beyond the Mediterranean to trade along the North Atlantic coastlines. Archaeological evidence shows that tin had been exported from Cornish mines to the Mediterranean during the Bronze Age, for example, and at an early date communities in Brittany, Cornwall, Ireland, Wales, Scotland, and possibly Spain became connected by trade and sea-travel. The trade links between these 'Celtic' areas led to the sharing of culture and language. Such bonds were reinforced by the difficulties of land travel, particularly through mountainous and boggy terrain. Consequently, coastal communities often had stronger links with other coastal communities from which they were separated by miles of sea than they did with communities a short distance away by land. Given our reliance on land travel today, it can be hard to appreciate how important sea travel once was and how it affected the spatial awareness of those whose lives revolved around it. Yet even as late as the nineteenth century, some relatively remote parts of the British Isles mainland remained more closely connected by sea than by land.

The first Christian communities in Ireland probably date from the third or fourth century, established by traders from Gaul or the Mediterranean. Although the pattern and process of diffusion is unclear, what is certain is that Christianity spread along the western seaboard. As well as being shaped by the already developing Celtic culture, the Christian mission in these remote coastal regions was also influenced by the fact that they were outside, or on the fringes of, the Roman Empire. This meant that these Christian communities developed largely without the direct influence of the Roman Church, which, after the conversion of Constantine, became closely associated with the territories of the Roman Empire. As a result, Celtic Christianity – if it is possible to view it in such a unified way – looked more towards the eastern Mediterranean region than to Rome. The link between eastern and western monasticism is evident in the reference in Tirechán's 'Collections' in the ninth century *Book of Armagh* that St Patrick, the 'Apostle of Ireland', spent no fewer than thirty years in the 'isles of the Tyrrhenian sea' (west of Italy) on the island Aralensis, which is thought to refer to Lérins. While this is almost certainly factually incorrect, it nevertheless points to a deeper truth about the pivotal role played by monasteries in Gaul in spreading monasticism to the Celtic rim and shaping Celtic Christianity.

The implications of this were both ecclesiastical and theological. In terms of Church organisation, there was an absence of Roman-style Church structures and administration with bishops, dioceses, and parishes in Celtic areas. Instead, their primary units were monasteries, which operated with autonomy under the leadership of an abbot. One of the most influential, St Columba, sailed with twelve followers from Ireland to the west coast of Scotland in *c.*563, and, two years later, to the island of Iona, where he established a monastic community. This community was to have considerable influence in the spread of monasticism. Most notably, it was to Iona that the Christian King Oswald of Northumbria looked when he wished to set up an evangelistic monastery in his kingdom. As a result, in 635 Aidan led a group of twelve monks from Iona to found a community on Lindisfarne on the Northumberland coast.

Although it would be wrong to say there was such an entity as *the* Celtic Church, what is certainly the case is that Christianity as practised in the Celtic regions shared distinctive characteristics and created a sense of identity which was sometimes in tension with Roman ecclesiology and theology. This came to a head in 664 at the Synod of Whitby, particularly over the dating of Easter. It was after this gathering of Church leaders that the Roman calendar for calculating the date of Easter was adopted, as well as other Roman practices such as the monastic haircut or 'tonsure' (the Celtic tradition was to shave the front of the scalp, the Roman to shave the top of the scalp). By the twelfth century, the distinctive features of Celtic Christianity had largely been eroded in the British Isles.

A feature of Celtic Christianity was its engagement with the natural world. This is evident from ancient literature and artefacts, which indicate a high degree of interaction between Christianity and pre-Christian nature worship. Syncretism of this kind, when an emerging religion absorbs elements of pre-existing religion, is common. In the case of Celtic Christianity, the Celtic cross is the most obvious example, integrating the Christian symbol of Christ's crucifixion with a circle symbolising the sun. Given that daily life was deeply influenced by the terrain and weather, it is hardly surprising that many Celtic prayers refer to the natural world, almost certainly drawing on pre-Christian invocations for help from nature. One of the best-known is the 'Lorica [Breastplate] of St Patrick'. This is an ancient prayer for protection, which lists the sources a Christian can turn to for strength: the Trinitarian God, Christ, the angelic host, patriarchs, prophets, apostles, and the natural world – God's creation – including the sea:

> I arise today:
> In the might of Heaven;
> Splendour of the Sun;
> Whiteness of Snow;
> Irresistibleness of Fire;
> The swiftness of Lightning;
> The speed of Wind;
> Absoluteness of the Deep;
> Earth's stability;
> Rock's durability.[2]

The 'absoluteness' of the sea in Celtic thinking was shaped by the belief that the Atlantic Ocean, which bordered many Celtic regions, was part of the great wild primordial ocean surrounding the Earth. This view of the world shaped mind-sets. Those living in Ireland or the west coast of Britain were seen as living – quite literally – at the end of the world and on the edge of the waters of chaos.

The concept that the Earth was a flat disc surrounded by chaotic waters predates Christianity. The earliest known map of the world, found on a 2,500 year-old fragment of a Babylonian cuneiform, shows the Earth in this way, with Babylon at its centre. Later Christian maps, most notably the Hereford

Mappa Mundi which dates from *c.*1300, continued to have the same basic format, but now with Jerusalem, the place of Jesus' death and resurrection, at the centre. This was despite the fact that Plato argued that the Earth was spherical in the late fourth century BCE in his 'dialogue' *Phaedo*, while Aristotle provided the evidence for this, from the curvature of the Earth's shadow on the moon, and from the way the horizon changes as the observer changes position, in his cosmological treatise *On the Heavens*, written in 350 BCE.

The reason why the flat, disc-shaped view of the Earth, as in the Hereford *Mappa Mundi,* persisted for so long is theological. As Jerry Brotton puts it, 'This is a map of religious faith, with a symbolic centre [Jerusalem] and monstrous margins [ocean].'³ A particularly influential Christian text, which reinforced this view of the world, was *The Nature of Things*, written by Isidore, Bishop of Seville, in *c.*612-15. Isidore presented an explanation for the way the world is from a Christian theological perspective, and in doing so effectively Christianised what are now known as T-O maps. These maps, of which there are many examples, show the Earth as a disc surrounded by chaotic waters – the ocean – with the disc comprising three land masses (Europe, Asia, and Africa) separated by three waterways in the shape of a 'T'. The monks of Iona are known to have used Isidore's works and clearly took on board his theological world-view, so that 'demons were as close to them in the Ocean as they were to St Antony in the deserts of Egypt.'⁴ Despite the geographical knowledge acquired by classical scholars, as will be discussed later Christian T-O maps dominated European thinking about the Earth for centuries.

Remote coastal locations and islands were ideal for monasticism, because they provided solitude for the ascetic lifestyle but were also accessible by water to obtain supplies, and there were normally springs and rivers at hand for drinking water. Perhaps, also, they offered much deeper things to aid prayer and contemplation. Many of the early Christian mystics drawn to this way of life were influenced by Plato's philosophy (if not his geography), which used the image of the vastness of the sea to express the goal of mysticism, and which he described as 'turning towards the great sea of the beautiful.'⁵ Christian ascetics were attracted to this image, living their lives with the purpose of turning to the great beauty of God – of achieving 'mystical union' with God.

The ascetic pull to be near the sea is well-illustrated in Bede's *Life of St Cuthbert*, the hagiography of the much-revered prior and later Bishop of Lindisfarne whose shrine is in Durham Cathedral. Cuthbert withdrew from his community, eventually settling on Inner Farne and building a wall so that he could see only the sky. Bede also provides a wonderful account of how Cuthbert interacted with the sea. This took place when Cuthbert visited the monastic community at Coldingham founded by the nun St Aebbe, close to what is now known as St Abb's Head on the south east coast of Scotland. Bede writes of Cuthbert:

> Now one night, a brother of the monastery, seeing him [Cuthbert] go out alone, followed him privately to see what he should do. But he [Cuthbert], when he left the monastery, went down to the sea, which flows beneath, and going into it, until the water reached his neck and arms, spent the night praising God. When the dawn of the day approached, he came out of the water, and falling on his knees, began to pray again. Whilst he was doing this, two quadrupeds, called otters, came up from the sea, and, lying down before him on the sand, breathed upon his feet, and wiped them with their hair: after which, having received his blessing, they returned to their native element. Cuthbert himself returned home in time to join in the accustomed hymns with the other brethren.[6]

Mortifying the flesh by standing in cold water highlights another reason why monastics were drawn to be near the sea. The sea's association with death, monsters, and evil made remote coastal sites and islands spiritual battlegrounds for the devout to face their own demons. There is no better example of such a place than Skellig Michael. Located eight miles off the west coast of Ireland, this 'skellig' (the Gaelic for rock) is mysterious and alluring from the mainland, while close up it appears wild and inhospitable. Yet, remarkably, this island was the home of a monastic community for six hundred years. Any visitor today who braves the journey to Skellig Michael will leave wondering how monks could possibly wish to live in such a harsh environment. The answer, perhaps, lies in its name. In the Book of Revelation, the archangel St Michael leads God's forces to defeat Satan when there is war in Heaven. Skelling Michael is a site for spiritual warfare: a place for testing in the extreme.

There are only a handful of facts known about the island's monastic community, but they are enough to fire the imagination. The writer Geoffrey Moorhouse used this scant information to speculate about what life might have been like for the monks in his book *Sun Dancing*. This fictional history paints a vivid picture of the harsh monastic life, and the deep impact of living by faith on what was believed by its inhabitants to be, quite literally, the edge of the world. One of the island's extraordinary features is the remains of a hermitage just below the island's precipitous South Peak. As Moorhouse points out, simply getting to this inaccessible and exposed place is highly dangerous and requires rock-climbing skills. In *Sun Dancing*, Moorhouse speculates that one of its hermits, Aedh, was a member of the Culdees – followers of an obsessive ascetic, Mael Ruain. So severe was their lifestyle that Moorhouse imagines Aedh hallucinating due to exhaustion and semi-starvation, while facing his own demons in the form of sexual desire:

> Sometimes, exhausted after hours of prayer on his knees or standing crosfigel [arms outstretched, like Christ on the cross], he would sit relaxed against the mountain wall, and look out to sea until the visions began. Angelic figures that were both tender and voluptuous beckoned him to ecstasies that he had never known but did not want to forget, and now that he was alone he surrendered himself at last: he used the scourge to punish and not to subdue. He more than once thought to imitate Origen [who is reputed to have castrated himself] afterwards; just once took up the razor and ran his thumb along its blade. Guilt in what God had given him.[7]

Skellig Michael not only gives an insight into medieval monasticism and the compulsion to find a desert in the ocean, but it speaks of the true nature of Celtic Christianity. For those influenced by this tradition today, it is easy to regard its engagement with the nature in terms of finding inspiration through awe and wonder. However, the essence of early Celtic Christianity was not so much about sensing God through the beauty of the world, but an awareness of God's providence in the struggle for survival – both physical and spiritual. Through the eyes of those who lived with the constant threat of storms and starvation and facing their own demons, as Moorhouse graphically describes, the island was as much hostile and sometimes terrifying as it was a dramatic and spectacular home. For the early Celtic Christians, sensing the Creator was primarily about recognising their absolute dependence upon God as provider and saviour.

Today, the journey to Skellig Michael remains one where even the irreligious may offer a prayer or two along the way. After crossing rough seas, landing on a tiny jetty, ascending hundreds of stone steps up a precipitous slope, the visitor – or pilgrim – is rewarded by entering the remarkable settlement of dry-stone 'beehive' monastic cells. It is impossible not to be moved by an awareness of what generations of monks endured for their faith and shared, huddled together on the side of a cliff. The priest and poet David

Scott has written of his own pilgrimage to Skellig Michael, and describes the moment he entered the monastic settlement:

> …Stop.
> Breathe. Let in the peace, and if you don't kneel there
> where on earth will you kneel?[8]

Anyone who has visited Skellig Michael will know precisely what he means.

If asceticism drew Celtic Christians to the sea, so too did evangelism. Just as the Celts had received the gospel by sea, so they used their own navigational skills to continue the Christian mission. A particular spur for their evangelical zeal was a belief that they were living in the end times. Expectation of the Second Coming of Christ and the Day of Judgment is evident in the writings of St Paul, but dissipates in later writings in the New Testament. However, over the past two thousand years there have been numerous occasions of heightened expectation. One such was in the late fourth and early fifth centuries, inspired by the writings of Augustine and Jerome which had reached monastic communities in the British Isles. The very fact that Christianity had spread to what was believed to be the end of the Earth was taken as a sign that the Christian mission was nearly complete and so the end times were near. This provided the impetus for missionaries to spread the gospel to as many people as quickly possible to ensure their salvation.

There is a romanticised view that there was an 'age of the saints' in the fifth and sixth centuries when many holy men – and they were almost all men – evangelised the western coast of Britain and Ireland, travelling by sea. Their names are known to us today from churches and towns dedicated to them: Asaph, David, Dubricius, Endellion, German, Gwinear, Perran, Petroc, Probus, and Tydfil, to name but a few. They are not saints in the sense of being formally canonised by the Church – and this list includes Patrick. Rather, they are regarded as holy people who had a particular strong impact as missionaries, who brought Christianity to towns and villages and who tended to move on from place to place. Tradition has it that often their travels were not planned. These holy travellers, or *peregrinati*, would set off in a boat, and leave it to the tides, winds, and currents – what they believed to be divine providence – to lead them to their destination. This probably drew on the pre-Christian Celtic practice of 'trial by drifting', when a convicted criminal was set out to sea in a boat, and it was left to the forces of nature to determine whether the person survived or perished. *Peregrinatio* is about a physical journey that acts out an inner journey; shedding the safety and security of a home and family and, to quote Philip Sheldrake, to 'cast oneself upon the mystery of God symbolised by the uncontrolled and unpredictable elements of the sea.'[9]

While *peregrinatio pro Dei amore* – 'wandering for the love of God' – may have been the case for some, other *peregrinati* appear to have followed established trade routes. Whether the destination of their journey was deliberate or not, what is certainly the case is that between the fifth and ninth centuries these holy sailors established Christian communities far and wide. St Sampson, for example, who grew up in South Wales and spent much time in the monastic community on Caldey Island off Tenby, crossed the Bristol Channel to Padstow and then sailed to Brittany, where he became Bishop of Dol; while St Ninian, who established a monastic community at Whithorn in Galloway, is reported to have travelled as a missionary up the east coast of Scotland, possibly as far as Shetland. These and many other Christian missionaries made considerable use of sea travel.

The reach of the *peregrinati* is evident from writings of this period. One of the great early geographic texts, *Liber de Mensura Orbis Terrae* (*Measure of the Free World*), written in c.825 by an Irish monk, Dicuil, is based on the accounts of travelling monks and tells of islands north of Britain – probably the Faroes – inhabited by monks who had sailed from Ireland. The more adventurous of the *peregrinati* must have been highly competent sailors, and extraordinarily brave. Famously, the Celts sailed in coracles or currachs: wooden-framed boats covered in animal hides. Practically, they were light and easy to carry and were well suited to travelling in shallow coastal waters, as they sat on the surface of the water. Currachs pre-date Christianity, but, as is so often the case, the influence of a new religion can shape traditional thinking. Jonathan Wooding suggests that these vessels may have had a religious significance. He suggests that the use of dead animal skin was a symbol of mortality, and that journeying in boats was seen as symbolic of our journey from Earth to Heaven through the gates of death. Evidence for this is found in one of the most remarkable pieces of literature of the period, the ninth-century *Navigatio Sancti Brendani Abbatis* (*Voyage of Saint Brendan the Abbot*).

There is no doubt that the inspiration behind the *Navigatio* was a real person, the monk Brendan from Fenit on the coast of Kerry, who was an important *peregrinati* known to have travelled by sea to Britanny, Wales, Scotland, and the isles of St Kilda, the Hebrides, Orkney, and the Faroes. However, the *Navigatio* is no conventional travelogue. Rather, it is a theological work that mixes fact and fantasy and is littered with allusions to Christian liturgy and the liturgical year. It is an allegory of the Christian life – or probably more accurately the monastic life – presenting the discipline of continuous prayer and contemplation as a voyage through dangerous seas to another, tranquil place: the Promised Land of the Saints. When Brendan and his companions get near that Promised Land they have to get out of their skin-covered coracle and get into a wooden-hulled boat instead to make it to their final destination. This has been interpreted as an image of shedding mortality to reach our final destination beyond the grave. The *Navigatio* bears similarities to Homer's *Iliad* and *Odyssey*, and also to heroic Irish sea-voyage stories such as the *Voyage of Bran*, known as *immrama*. The imagery in the *Navigatio* voyage may well refer to places visited by various *peregrinati*, including Brendan. If so, their reach was extensive. References to fauna suggest the 'Island of Sheep' is in the Faroes, the 'fiery islands' may refer to the volcanoes of Iceland, the 'crystal pillar' may well be icebergs off Greenland, and references to fog suggest Newfoundland, and flowers and grapes may point to the 'Promised Land' being Florida.

The possibility of sailing across the Atlantic in a currach was put to the test in the 1970s by Tim Severin. Wanting to find out whether the voyage described in the *Navigatio* was feasible, Severin constructed a sailing boat, the *Brendan*, with a timber-framed hull covered in leather. The plan was to set sail from Brendan Creek, on the Dingle Peninsula of Ireland, on St Brendan's feast day, 16 May 1976. However, poor weather delayed the departure until the following day. One year and six weeks later, on 26 June 1977, the *Brendan* reached Peckford Island,150 miles north of St John's, Newfoundland, having crossed three and a half thousand miles of ocean. Commenting on the medieval monks who may have made a similar journey over a thousand years earlier, Severin said, 'Such men must have been special people, even by the exacting standards of their own day.'[10]

The Anglo-Saxon poem 'The Seafarer', from the tenth-century *Exeter Book* held at Exeter Cathedral, gives insight into what the *peregrinati* endured. While some scholars regard the poem's narrator as an old sailor, others see him as a hermit seeking a desert in the ocean. Whatever interpretation is correct, the opening lines of 'The Seafarer' evokes a sense of the harshness of being alone at sea:

> I of myself can a true tale relate,
> my fortune recount, how I, in days of toil,
> a time of hardship oft suffer'd,

bitter-breast cares have endure'd
prov'd in the ship strange mishaps many.
The fell rolling of the waves
has me there oft drench'd;
on anxious night-watch, at the vessel's prow,
when on the cliff it strikes[11]

Yet despite the dangers and privations the poem also gives a sense of what the seafarer was seeking:

Let us consider where we may have a home,
and then think how we may thither come,
and then also prepare ourselves,
that we may go thereto into the eternal happiness,
where life depends on the Lord's love, joy in heaven;
therefore be to the Holy thanks,
that he us hath honour'd, the Chief of glory,
the Lord eternal, in all time.[12]

Travel by sea, then, was both a way of spreading the gospel and putting faith to the test, with the ultimate objective of bringing oneself and others to what the *Navigatio* calls the 'Promised Land' and what The Seafarer calls 'home'.

While monastic and evangelistic *peregrinati* were sailing west in search of solitude or souls to save, another type of *peregrinati* were travelling the opposite direction. The fourth century saw the birth of Christian pilgrimage, when Christians from afar began to visit the Holy Land and the places familiar to Jesus and his disciples, with Jerusalem the ultimate destination, as emphasised by its centrality on T-O maps. These pilgrims travelled by land or sea, or often by a combination of both.

The best-known early pilgrim is Egeria, thought to be a Spanish nun, who travelled to the Holy Land at the end of the fourth century. It is interesting to note the Bishop of Edessa's observation on her journey from Spain when he welcomed her with the words, 'My daughter, I can see what a long journey this is on which your faith has brought you – right from the other end of the earth.'[13] Behind this lies the thought that the waters beyond Spain – the Atlantic – was the edge of the world.

Only the middle section of Egeria's account remains, so we have no description of her journey to and from the Holy Land. Other, later, descriptions do exist, however. In *The Spring Voyage*, R. J. Mitchell cleverly recreates a travelogue of a medieval pilgrimage to Jerusalem, using the independent accounts of several *peregrinati*. One feature that stands out is the hazardous and arduous nature of the voyages between Venice, which became a major port for pilgrims, and Joppa (now known as Jaffa), the nearest coastal city to Jerusalem. The threat of pirates and corsairs, storms, and the discomfort of life on board ship all took their toll on the pilgrims. Mitchell comments wryly that an uncomfortable and dangerous voyage was an integral part of the pilgrimage, and for the pilgrims it 'made their whole enterprise seem more meritorious'.[14] Perhaps it did looking back, but maybe at the time their feelings were less pious. Describing the return of fellow pilgrims to Venice after a particularly difficult voyage to Venice, Roberto da Sansaverino observed:

> With the grace of God and of the most glorious Virgin his Mother, they left the ship and reached the shore … as though they had come out of darkness into light, leaving hell and returning to paradise … they felt great pleasure, joy, contentment and consolation – at finding themselves on dry land – than ever before in their lives.[15]

Others were less fortunate. In 1102, an English pilgrim, Saewulf – who had survived seven days and nights of being on a ship tossed by storms – witnessed twenty-three ships crash into reefs off Jaffa, drowning more than a thousand pilgrims.[16] No wonder pilgrims wrote their wills before setting off.

Alongside the desire to visit holy places was the even greater compulsion to control them. While early Christian pilgrims travelled to the Holy Land in peace, things began to change after the rise of Islam, particularly after Jerusalem was besieged and came under Muslim control in 638. Eventually, this led to two centuries of conflict – the Crusades – in which Church-backed military raids sought to bring the Holy Land under Christian rule. The Crusades created another type of *peregrinati*: *milites peregrini* or *pergreni crucesignati* – Crusaders – many of whom travelled by sea to fight for Christendom. The changing nature of pilgrimage is exemplified in the story of the Hospitallers. This religious order was founded by Italian merchants in the eleventh century to run a hospital in Jerusalem to care for sick and poor pilgrims, under the leadership of a monk called Gerard. After the First Crusade wrested Jerusalem from Muslim control in 1099, the Hospitallers extended their work around the Mediterranean along main pilgrim routes. They also took on a military role and a new name: the Order of St John of Jerusalem. After the recapture of Jerusalem by Muslim forces in 1197, the

Order relocated its headquarters to Cyprus, and then later to Rhodes and eventually to Malta. In doing so, the Order became increasingly involved in shipping, both in transporting pilgrims and Crusaders, until, eventually, it was running a private navy.

The Order's fleet of galleys, which sailed through the eastern Mediterranean and coast of North Africa in order to capture Muslim shipping, was a far cry from the simple currach that had taken monks to search for their desert in the ocean. The sea had become not only a spiritual battlefield, but a military one as well – and all in the name of religion.

1   (Trans. T. Vivian, K. Vivian and J. Burton Russell) *The Lives of the Jura Fathers* (Kalamazoo: Cistercian Publications, 1999), p. 197.
2   Greg Tobin, *The Wisdom of St Patrick: Inspirations from the Patron Saint of Ireland* (New York: Ballantine Books, 1999), p. 229.
3   Jerry Brotton, *A History of the World in Twelve Maps* (London: Penguin, 2012), p. 90.
4   Thomas O'Loughlin, 'Living in the Ocean', in Cormac Bourke (ed.), *Studies in the Cult of Saint Columba* (Dublin: Four Courts Press, 1997), p. 13.
5   McGinn, 'Ocean and Desert', pp. 157-8.
6   *The Ecclesiastical History of the English Nation by the Venerable Bede* (London: J.M. Dent, 1910), p. 301.
7   Geoffrey Moorhouse, *Sun Dancing: A Medieval Vision* (London: Phoenix, 1998), p. 84.
8   David Scott, *Beyond the Drift: New and Selected Poems* (Hexham: Bloodaxe Books, 2015), p. 180.
9   Philip Sheldrake, *Living Between Worlds: Place and Journey in Celtic Spirituality* (London: Darton, Longman and Todd, 1995), p. 59.
10 Tim Severin, *The Brendan Voyage: The Greatest Adventure of the Sea since Kon-Tiki* (London: Arrow, 1978), pp. 232-3.
11 Benjamin Thorpe, *Codex Exoniensis: A Collection of Anglo-Saxon Poetry* (London: Society of Antiquaries of London, 1842), p. 306.
12 Ibid., pp. 312-3.
13 John Wilkinson, *Egeria's Travels* (Warminster: Aris and Phillips, 1999), p. 133.
14 R.J. Mitchell, *The Spring Voyage: The Jerusalem Pilgrimage in 1458* (London: John Murray, 1965), p. 71.
15 Ibid., p. 175.
16 David Jacoby, 'Ports of pilgrimage to the Holy Land, Eleventh-Fourteenth Century: Jaffa, Acre, Alexandria', in *The Holy Portolano: The Sacred Geography of Navigation in the Middle Ages* (Berlin: De Gruyter, 2014), pp. 51-2.

5

To Unpathed Waters,
Undreamed Shores

Disturb us, Lord, to dare more boldly, to venture on
wider seas, where storms will show your mastery,
where losing sight of land, we shall find the stars.
                                              Sir Francis Drake

In European history, the late-fifteenth and early-sixteenth centuries are
often regarded as the close of one era and the beginning of another. A date
which is sometimes seen as pivotal to bringing the Middle Ages to a close
and starting the Early Modern period is 12 October 1492. The reason for
such precise timing is that on this day, having sailed across the Atlantic, the
Italian explorer Christopher Columbus landed on an island in the Bahamas
called by its own people Guanahani, which he gave the name San Salvador
(Holy Saviour). The 'age of discovery' was well and truly under way, and
with it came a period of European empire-building and associated political
struggles, wars, fervent Christian mission, and a changed perception of global
geography. No wonder, then, that this date is seen as a watershed.

Christopher Columbus was not the first European to reach the Americas.
As already discussed, the *Navigatio* suggests that Europeans may have reached
Newfoundland and possibly Florida sometime before the ninth century. The
fourteenth-century Icelandic *Saga of Erik the Red* refers to the Norse explorer
Leif Erikson establishing a settlement in Vinland, which is thought to be
Newfoundland, at the beginning of the eleventh century. The saga, which
may owe something to the influence of the *Navigatio*, tells of Leif sailing from
Norway to return home to Greenland under the instruction of King Olaf
Tryggvason to 'preach Christianity' to the pagan Norse settlers. Leif's ship
went off-course, taking him to 'lands of which before he had no expectation'

where there were 'fields of wild wheat, and the vine-tree in full growth' and 'trees which were called maples'. Before he returned to Greenland, the saga says of Leif, 'Thus did he show his great munificence and his graciousness when he brought Christianity to the land, and saved the shipwrecked crew. He was called "Leif the Lucky".'[1] This story was given credence in the early 1960s by the discovery of eleventh-century Viking houses at L'Anse aux Meadows on the northern tip of Newfoundland.

While Leif's adventure was the stuff of legend and saga, it is also plausible that less celebrated Europeans set foot on North American soil centuries before Columbus. Again, this was a consequence of Christianity, but this time due to the economic forces of supply and demand rather than mission. One of the lesser-known consequences of the Reformation was that the rise of Protestantism in Europe greatly reduced the practice of fasting by not eating meat. Fasting during Lent was a practice developed early in Christianity, as was fasting on Fridays in remembrance of Christ's death on Good Friday. Advent also became a season of fasting, and the practice was extended to numerous saint days and other Christian festivals, so much so that by the thirteenth and fourteenth centuries the fast days imposed by the Roman Catholic Church accounted for more than half the days of the year. Fasting on this scale created an enormous demand for fish, the preferred food for those abstaining from meat. As a result, fishing expeditions went further out to sea in search of new fishing grounds, and by 1510 Europeans are known to have been fishing off Newfoundland. Brian Fagan suggests that some Europeans may have been fishing in this area much earlier, and possibly reached land.[1] It is therefore possible that the first Europeans to reach North America, if not Norse sailors, were monks or fishermen. What is certain is that they were not explorers from 'the age of discovery'.

The significance of Columbus' first voyage across the Atlantic in 1492 is not so much its pioneering nature (though at the time, of course, it was seen in these terms) but rather its purpose and consequence. Sponsored by the Spanish monarchs Ferdinand II and Isabella I, the expedition was about discovery – not primarily for the sake of adventure or curiosity, but for the potential for acquiring wealth, developing trade, building an empire, and competing for maritime supremacy with Portugal (though intriguingly, Columbus had initially approached King John II of Portugal to fund the voyage, but without success).

Columbus was one of several pioneering sailors of the period who began to expand European ambitions and change perceptions of geography. In 1434, Cape Bogador (or Bojador) on the west coast of Africa was crossed in a voyage sponsored by Henry the Navigator of Portugal, proving that land lay beyond what many regarded as the end of land in the south – albeit some 2,000 years after the Phoenicians had circumnavigated Africa, according to the Greek historian Herodotus, writing in the fifth century BCE. By 1488 the Cape of Good Hope had also been rounded, perhaps for the first time since the Phoenicians. While political and economic ambitions were undoubtedly important driving forces behind these expeditions, there was also a religious dimension. The potential for Christian mission was a significant factor, and so too was the motivation to find a sea route to Asia in order for Europeans to connect and unite with a Christian Church believed to exist in a land cut off from the rest of Christendom by Muslim territories and ruled by a Christian king, Prester John.

For Columbus, however, there was an additional religious impetus. Like many Celtic *peregrinati* before him, Columbus was deeply influenced by millennialism. Columbus believed that he was living in the end times, when a new cosmic order – 'new heavens and a new earth' (Isaiah 65:17) – would be established by God through the Second Coming of Christ, who would reign for 1,000 years. Columbus' library includes a copy of Pierre d'Ailly's *Imago Mundi*. Written in 1410, this compendium of cosmology and geography also contains apocalyptic theology. The *Imago Mundi* and other medieval eschatological theological works, such as those of Joachim of Fiore, clearly influenced Columbus and led him to the belief that the end of the world was imminent. More than that, Columbus believed he was called by God to play a prominent role in bringing about this cosmic reordering. Behind Columbus' transatlantic expedition of 1492-3 and subsequent expeditions in 1493-6, 1498-1500, and 1502-4, was, as one biographer puts it, 'an unmistakable sense of mission and apostolic election.'[2] This is evident when, toward the end of his life, Columbus began to refer to himself using a Latin variant of his name, 'Christoferens', which means 'Christ-bearer'.

The impact of apocalyptic theology on Columbus is most apparent in his extraordinary *Book of Prophecies*, written in 1501-2, after his third transatlantic voyage, with the help of a Carthusian monk, Fr Gaspar de Gorritto. In this book, Columbus seeks to justify his transatlantic expeditions from a theological perspective, beginning with a personal account of his sense of divine calling to be an explorer:

> At a very early age I began sailing the sea and have continued until now ... Our Lord has favoured my occupation and has given me an intelligent mind. He has endowed me with a great talent for seamanship;

sufficient ability in astrology, geometry, and arithmetic; and the mental and physical dexterity required to draw spherical maps of cities, rivers and mountains, islands and ports, with everything in its proper place.

   During this time I have studied all kinds of texts: cosmography, histories, chronicles, philosophy, and other disciplines. Through these writings, the hand of Our Lord opened my mind to the possibility of sailing to the [East] Indies and gave me the will to attempt the voyage… Who could doubt that this flash of understanding was the work of the Holy Spirit, as well my own? The Holy Spirit illuminated his holy and sacred Scripture, encouraged me in a very strong and clear voice from the forty books of the Old Testament, the four evangelists, and twenty-three epistles from the blessed apostles, arguing me to proceed. Continually, without ceasing, they insisted that I go on.[3]

In Columbus' apocalyptic thought-world, several pre-conditions needed to be met before the cosmic reordering of 'new heavens and a new earth' would come about. First, Christianity must spread 'to the ends of the earth' in fulfilment of Christ's great commission: 'Go therefore and make disciples of all nations' (Matthew 28:19). Like *peregrinati* before him, Columbus saw himself as a missionary, prepared to risk danger in order to spread the gospel to the ends of the Earth. In the *Book of Prophecies*, Columbus repeatedly quotes Psalm 19:4: 'their voice goes out through all the earth, / and their words to the end of the world.' A second requirement was to rediscover the lost paradise of the Garden of Eden. Just as Eden was central to the fall of humanity, in the apocalyptical mind-set it was also central to humanity's final salvation, but nobody knew where it was. Eden, it was thought, had become an island, separated from the rest of land by water after the Flood, and its location was unknown but to the east. Again, Columbus saw himself as destined to have a role as the explorer who would rediscover paradise – something he believed he achieved during his third transatlantic voyage, when he reached the Gulf of Paria on west coast of the island which he named Trinidad, after the Holy Trinity.

   A third prerequisite for the apocalypse was that the Holy Land should be under Christian rule, in preparation for the return of Christ to Jerusalem. To achieve this, Columbus believed it was necessary to mount a final crusade to free the Holy Land from Muslim control, an expedition Columbus referred to in the *Book of Prophecies* as 'the voyage to the Holy Sepulchre' – the place where Christ was crucified, died, and resurrected. This territorial mind-set was undoubtedly influenced by recent events. It was within Columbus' lifetime that the great Christian city of Constantinople was captured by the Ottoman Turks and became part of the Muslim-controlled Ottoman Empire, with its magnificent cathedral, the Hagia Sophia, converted into a mosque.

The expansion of the Ottoman Empire and capture of Constantinople rekindled a crusading zeal which Columbus shared, with Jerusalem – the holiest site of all – the main focus. A crusade to recapture Jerusalem, Columbus argued, could be funded by wealth acquired from Asia, particularly gold and spices. Like many others, Columbus was familiar with the *Travels of Marco Polo* who, although he never visited Japan (which he called Zipangu), wrote of the Japanese, 'Their religion is the worship of idols' and 'They have gold in the greatest abundance, its source being inexhaustible.'[4] The best way to access this wealth (and convert the idolaters) was, Columbus believed, to avoid the dangers of travelling eastwards, which would involve passing through the Muslim-controlled Ottoman Empire, and instead establish a trade route to Asia – not by sailing east, but by sailing west.

While Columbus was well aware that the Earth was spherical, his world-view was influenced by the cosmology underpinning T-O maps. These Christocentric maps, orientated for theological reasons, placed Jerusalem at their centre. They also included only the three land masses: Asia, Africa and Europe – something apparently supported by Genesis 9:19: 'The sons of Noah who went out of the ark were Shem, Ham, and Japheth … and from these the whole earth was peopled.' Shem, who was believed to be the oldest son of Noah, was associated with populating the largest continent, Asia; Ham with Africa; and Japheth with Europe (see Figure 2).

In planning his expedition, Columbus had no conception that there might be another land mass between Europe and Asia. Instead, he believed that by sailing west he would eventually reach Asia. It is for this reason that, after leaving the Bahamas on his first transatlantic voyage, Columbus set off in search of Japan, and on reaching Cuba believed he had reached Cathay (part of what is now known as China) on the Asian mainland – a view he firmly maintained despite growing evidence to the contrary. Columbus had no desire to 'discover' a new continent. His objective as an explorer was to find a route to Asia for theological reasons explained in a letter written towards the end of his life:

> God made me the messenger of the new heaven and the new earth of which he spoke in the Apocalypse of St John after having spoken of it through the mouth of Isaiah; and he showed me the spot where to find it.[5]

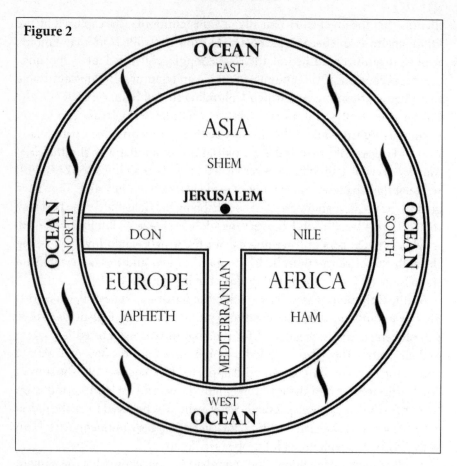

Figure 2

Columbus, then, saw himself the fulfiller of prophecy who was helping to inaugurate a new age – a self-perception largely ignored in popular history, in which he is portrayed instead as a pioneering explorer in search of new lands.

Columbus was not alone in crossing the Atlantic at this time. In 1496 another Italian, John Cabot, sailed from Bristol on board the *Matthew* in an expedition sponsored by Henry VII of England, and landed in Newfoundland. Cabot was perhaps the first European to set foot on North American soil since the Vikings – unless he was beaten to it by unknown fishermen. Then, in 1500, the Portuguese explorer Pedro Álvares Cabral landed in what was later named Brazil – a name probably taken from brazilwood rather than, as once thought, hy-Brasil, a mythical island thought to exist somewhere in the Atlantic west of Ireland. In 1519, the Spanish conquistador Hernán Cortés sailed from Cuba (which he had assisted Diego Velázquez in conquering in 1511) and subjugated Mexico. While between 1519 and 1522, the Portuguese explorer Ferdinand Magellan led an expedition across the Atlantic and Pacific. Magellan was killed during a battle in the Philippines, but others completed the expedition to become the first recorded people to circumnavigate the globe.

These journeys of discovery had profound consequences. They led to the building of empires, the establishment of colonies, the subjugation of indigenous peoples, and the world-wide spread of Christianity. They also changed the European mind-set, a process Barry Cunliffe has described as 'a dramatic and unsettling shift in cognitive geography.'[6] In the past, Europeans looked primarily landwards and eastwards; to the west lay the fearful and dangerous unknown of the Atlantic. Within a couple of generations this had all changed. Europeans were now looking seawards in all directions, not least westwards. The Atlantic, which had previously been the territory of the brave few, became the link between the Old World and the New. The western horizon no longer spoke fearfully of the unknown, but enticingly of potential and opportunity.

Europe, it has been said, 'burst its bonds' in the sixteenth century.[7] The pace of European colonialism after the expeditions of Columbus and others was rapid. Soon vast areas of the Americas and Africa were colonised by European countries, who also established trading outposts in Asia. This expansion paved the way for Christian missionaries as contact was made with indigenous peoples, and the consequence of this was dramatic. In the sixteenth century, European sea power made Christianity a global religion.

With the Reformation in its infancy and focused within Europe, most missionary activity in this period was Roman Catholic; Protestant mission was a later phenomenon. The appearance of missionary priests disembarking from ships must have instilled a range of emotions in those who first saw them, ranging from terror to excitement. Such diverse feelings would have been justified, as the attitude and approach of missionaries could be very different. A common approach of missionaries was to establish Christian communities that included a church, school, hospital, and orphanage. The more enlightened sought to achieve this by working with the cultures of indigenous peoples; others did so by imposing harsh and brutal regimes.

One of the first countries to receive Christian missionaries at this time was India. In 1497, the Portuguese explorer Vasco da Gama reached this prized destination by sailing east, around the Cape of Good Hope and across the Indian Ocean, taking with him a team of priests. Soon after establishing a base in India, the Portuguese became aware of the existence of St Thomas Christians, who traced their origins back to the missionary activity of Thomas the Apostle. Like the mythical Christians under the equally mythical Prester John, the St Thomas Christians were disconnected from Christians elsewhere. While initial contact was friendly, it rapidly became difficult and complex as the Roman Catholic Church sought to bring the St Thomas Christians under the authority of the Pope, leading to a fracturing of relations. Ecumenism was not an option.

India was also one of the first countries to receive Jesuit missionaries. The Society of Jesus (the Jesuits) was established in 1540 as a Christian militia devoted to the conversion of pagans and reconversion of heretics. The Pope and the King of Portugal were quick to commission one of the Society's founders, the Basque missionary St Francis Xavier, to develop missionary activity in the East. On 7 April 1541, Francis sailed from Lisbon on board the *Santiago*. After a seven-month stopover in Mozambique, he reached the Indian island of Goa on 6 May 1542, where he established a mission. As well as preaching, teaching, and ministering to the sick, Francis proposed setting up a Goa Inquisition, to stop and punish heresy against Christianity. The Inquisition was not established until 1560, eight years after Francis' death, but it has left a stain on this saint's reputation. The inquisition's treatment of those brought to trial – particularly of supposed crypto-Hindus – was brutal, involving imprisonment, floggings, and executions.

The experience of the Indian mission was replicated elsewhere as sea travel enabled Christianity to spread across the globe. The complex mixture of disregard for other faiths, domination and persecution, deeply ambiguous attitudes towards indigenous cultures, and a strong desire to provide spiritual and physical care and education in the name of Christ, has left an enduring and confusing legacy. While the colonialism of the age of discovery is now widely and rightly regarded as abhorrent, Christianity has taken hold in many colonised countries and is now an important part of their culture. Ironically, while the colonial powerhouse of Western Europe has now become the most secular region of the world, parts of Central and South America, Africa and Asia colonised and Christianised by European countries in the 'age of discovery' have witnessed the most rapid growth of Christianity in recent times.

⌒

While the age of discovery had significant consequences for the spread of Christianity, it also had considerable theological implications. For centuries, the proven classical concept of the Earth as a globe had co-existed with a Christian cosmology as expressed in T-O maps, in which the ocean was perceived as the remnant of primordial chaos on the edge of the world and of little practical use to humanity. This curious co-existence of two conflicting geographical concepts came to an end when Columbus and others provided clear information about the oceans, how they interconnected, and how, in the words of Steve Mentz, they could be 'a space for human activity, risk and opportunity.'[8]

The person who, perhaps more than anyone else, popularised the new geographical understanding of the world was an English priest, Richard Hakluyt. Known as 'the father of modern geography', Hakluyt sought out sea captains, sailors, and merchants to glean information about their travels. These accounts provided Hakluyt with material for the public lectures he delivered at Oxford University and for his writings, including *The Principall Navigations, Voiages and Discoveries of the English Nation*, published in 1588. This book proved highly influential, and not only among geographers and sailors.

One of those inspired by Hakluyt was William Shakespeare. In his play *The Winter's Tale*, the character Camillo speaks of the risky opportunity of sailing 'To unpathed waters, undreamed shores'. As well as capturing the spirit of the age of discovery, Shakespeare was also attuned to the deeper questions it posed. As Dan Brayton puts it, 'Coming to terms with the vastness of a blue planet had enormous implications for thinking about humanity's place in the cosmos, and Shakespeare's writings reflect this conceptual challenge.'[9] Shakespeare's references to the sea are both literal and metaphorical. His literal use, including the shipping trade of *The Merchant of Venice* and shipwrecks in *The Winter's Tale*, *The Tempest*, and *Twelfth Night*, express something of the importance of sea travel and dangers of life at sea. More intriguing, however, is the way Shakespeare employs sea imagery to speak of the human condition. Shakespeare writes as if the sea's varying moods and temperament mirror our own. The 'angered ocean' of *Antony and Cleopatra*, the 'roaring sea' of *King Lear*, the 'ambitious ocean' of *Julius Caesar*, or the 'wild and wasteful ocean' of *Henry V* suggest a deep bond – perhaps of a spiritual nature – between humanity and the sea. This is stark contrast to the disconnect implied in Genesis, where the sea is the remnant of the pre-creation state, while humanity is the 'crown of all creation', as the Church of England's current Eucharistic liturgy expresses it.[10]

The extent and accuracy of Shakespeare's use of nautical terminology in his plays led the English scholar A.F. Falconer to propose that he spent some of his 'lost years' (for which there is no firm biographical information) serving as a sailor in Elizabeth I's navy during the war with Spain. 'One thing can be taken as certain, it was during this period that Shakespeare came to know the sea and the navy' asserts Falconer, who served as a naval officer during the Second World War.[11] An alternative and more consistent explanation, which Falconer disputed, is that Shakespeare was particularly well-informed by the writings of Hakluyt and others.

A contemporary of Shakespeare who certainly did have first-hand experience of being at sea was the poet and priest John Donne. While in his mid-twenties, Donne served in the Royal Navy as a gentleman-volunteer during the Anglo-Spanish War, first in an expedition to capture Cádiz from the Spanish in 1596, and then, in the following year, as part of a failed attempt to occupy the Azores. These experiences had a profound effect on Donne who, like Shakespeare, made frequent literal and metaphorical use of the sea and sailing in his poetry. The inspiration for his poems 'Storm' and 'Calm', for example, came from experiencing a terrifying storm and then being becalmed during the Azores expedition.

Exploration fascinated Donne, who drew on its imagery to powerful effect. In 'The Good Morrow', two lovers delight in discovering a 'new world' in each other:

> Let sea-discoverers to new worlds have gone,
> Let maps to others, worlds on worlds have shown,
> Let us possess one world, each hath one, and is one.

In one of his most erotic poems, 'Love's Progress', Donne likens the intensity of sexual desire to the almost obsessive drive in people such as Columbus to embark on dangerous voyages to discover new routes to Asia. Like being at sea, being in love can involve experiencing storms and sickness; and just as a voyage can lead to a prized, exotic destination, so too can exploring a lover's body. The imagery Donne uses is highly sensuous. Beginning with her brow (which 'becalms us when 'tis smooth and plain, / And when 'tis wrinkled, shipwrecks us again'), the poet works his way down past her lips ('a creek of safe anchor'), her breasts ('Sestos and Abydos flanking the Hellespont'), her abdomen ('a boundless sea' with 'island moles'), to the final, exotic, and highly desirable destination of 'her India'.

Later in life, when Donne was an Anglican priest and Dean of St Paul's, he used similar imagery in his religious poetry. In the poem 'Hymn to God my God, in my Sickness', written when he was dying, Donne returned to the same metaphor as in 'Love's Progress'. This time, however, the 'voyage' is not one of erotic love but towards death; and it is not a lover who is exploring a body but doctors, who are seeking to diagnose Donne's illness:

> Whilst my physicians by their love are grown
> Cosmographers, and I their map, who lie
> Flat on this bed, that by them may be shown
> That this is my south-west discovery,
> *Per fretum febris*, by these straits to die.

The 'south-west discovery' is an allusion to the Pacific Ocean. In 1519 Magellan sailed down the east coast of South America and through what became known as the Magellan Strait – a navigable sea route in southern Chile that links the Atlantic and Pacific oceans. Donne drew on Magellan's voyage to speak about his impending death. As Malcolm Guite interprets the poem, Donne is travelling from the Atlantic, the western ocean associated with the setting sun and death, to the Pacific, the eastern ocean associated with the rising sun and resurrection. Donne is telling himself that his impending death is the route to the resurrection life: 'Be this my text, my sermon to mine own: / "Therefore that he may raise, the Lord throws down."'[12]

Donne, famed in his day as preacher as much as poet, includes powerful allusions to the sea in his sermons, such as the following preached at The Hague:

> The world is a sea in many respects and assimilations. It is a sea as it is subject to storms and tempests; every man (and every man is a world) feels that ... It is a sea as it is bottomless to any line which we can sound it with, and endless to any discovery that we can make of it ... It is a sea as it hath ebbs and floods, and no man knows the true reason of those floods and those ebbs ... It is a sea as the sea affords water enough for all the world to drink, but such water as will not quench the thirst ... It is a sea if we consider the inhabitants. In the sea the greater fish devour the less, and so do the men of this world, too.[13]

Sea voyages into the unknown, and settling in unfamiliar lands beyond the horizon, evoked in Donne a sense of passing from this world into the next. And so, in the sermon, Donne continues, 'All these wayes the world is a Sea', which then leads into the main point of the metaphor:

> but especially it is a Sea in this respect, the Sea is no place of habitation, but a passage to our habitations. So the Apostle expresses the world, *Here we have no continuing City, but we seek one to come*; we seeke it

not here, but we seeke it whilest we are here, els we shall never finde it. Those are the two great works which we are to doe in this world; first to know, that this world is not our home, and then to provide us another home, whilest we are in this world.[14]

The idea of the world not being our 'home' is fraught with dangers. It can lead to a disregard for the planet from an environmental point of view, as ultimately it is dispensable, and similarly towards those of other faiths and cultures who need to be directed to their true home. Today, the former issue is of particular concern as we are caught-up in an environmental crisis. However, we also have to face the consequences of the latter, in terms of addressing the legacy of colonialism, and the role played by people such as Donne.

In 1622, when Dean of St Paul's, Donne was made an honorary member of the Virginia Company of London. Founded in 1606 to establish British colonial settlements in North America, the 'Conversion of Virginians' was also part of the Company's remit. Donne addressed this in the Company's annual sermon on 13 November 1622, when he preached on the text, 'you will receive power when the Holy Spirit has come upon you; and you will be my witnesses in Jerusalem, in all Judea and Samaria, and to the ends of the earth' (Acts 1:8). Donne drew parallels between the work of the Company and Christ's apostles and gives a sense of the emerging Protestant attitude towards colonialism:

> the *Acts* of the *Apostles* were to convay that name of *Christ Jesus*, and to propagate his *Gospell*, over all the world: Beloved, you are *Actors* upon the same Stage too: the uttermost part of the Earth are your *Scene*: act over the *Acts* of the *Apostles*; bee you a light to the *Gentiles*, that sit in darknesse; be you content to carry him over these *Seas*, who dryed up one *Red Sea* for his first people, and hath powred out another *red Sea*, his owne bloud, for them and us.[15]

Donne then develops the idea of mission in terms of sea voyage, where:

> as *God* taught us to build houses, not to house our selves, but to house him, in erecting *Churches*, to his glory: So *God* taught us to make Ships, not to transport our selves, but to transport him, *That when wee have received power, after that the Holy Ghost is come upon us, we might be witnesses unto him, both in Jerusalem, and in all* Judæa *and in* Samaria, *and unto the uttermost parts of the Earth.*[16]

The sermon concludes with a passive-aggressive call for the Company to convert native Americans:

> inflame them with your *godlinesse*, and your *Religion*. Bring them to *love* and *Reverence* the name of that *King*, that sends men to teache them the ways of *Civilitie* in this world, but to *feare* and *adore* the Name of that *King of Kings*, that sends men to teach them the waies of Religion, for the next world... You shall add persons to this Kingdome, and to the Kingdome of heaven, and adde names to the Bookes of our Chronicles, and to the Booke of Life.[17]

While Donne was involved in colonialism from the perspective of the State Church – the Church of England – it was a group of Christians who had split from the Church of England, known as separatists, who came to symbolise the opportunity afforded by sea travel across the Atlantic. Deeply influenced by Calvinism, the separatists were one of many protestant groups that opposed state involvement in religion. Consequently, their activities were made illegal and they faced persecution. In around 1607 a group of separatists migrated to Holland and settled in Leiden as members of the English Separatist Church. However, fearing the loss of their religious and cultural identity as they became integrated in Dutch society, the decision was taken to relocate and found a colony in which they would be free to practise their religion and where they could retain their cultural identity.

The separatists struck a deal with the London Company, which had been founded in 1606 to establish colonies in North America, and in 1620 a group of them migrated from Leiden. The separatists sailed to Southampton on board the *Speedwell* to meet the second ship involved in the voyage, the *Mayflower*. After setting sail, the *Speedwell* began to take on water, and after both ships were diverted to Dartmouth for the *Speedwell* to be inspected, she was deemed unseaworthy. Then, on 16 September, the *Mayflower* set sail from Plymouth on a 66 day voyage, during which those on board experienced violent Atlantic storms. The intention was to land in Northern Virginia, but having been driven further north the first land spotted was Cape Cod. It proved too dangerous to sail south, and so it was agreed to anchor in what is now Provincetown Harbor and for the new colony to be established in the area they called Plymouth.

The voyage of the *Mayflower* has come to symbolise the 'American Dream' of freedom and opportunity, with its role in American history taking on almost mythic status much later when those on board came to be known as the Pilgrim Fathers. In the only written account by someone on board the

Mayflower, the separatist William Bradford, who became Governor of the Plymouth Colony, described their arrival at Provincetown:

> Being thus arrived in a good harbour, and brought safely to land, they fell upon their knees and blessed the God of heaven who had brought them over the vast and furious ocean, and delivered them from all the perils and miseries thereof, again to set their feet on the firm and stable earth, their proper element.
>
> Having thus passed the vast ocean, and a sea of troubles before in their preparation, they had now no friends to welcome them, nor inns to entertain or refresh their weather-beaten bodies, no houses or, much less, towns to repair to, to seek for succor... If they looked behind them there was the mighty ocean which they had passed, and which was now a barrier and gulf to separate them from all the civilized world.[18]

Such was the power of the separatists' story of overcoming adversity in search of opportunity and freedom that, in 1863, while the American Civil War was raging, President Abraham Lincoln proclaimed a national Thanksgiving Day in their honour. Thanksgiving Day has become a significant national holiday in the Unites States, commemorating the three day feast organised by Bradford in November 1621 that the colonists shared with local Native Americans to celebrate their first harvest after settling in New England. Lincoln's decision to enshrine this commemoration in law cemented the Pilgrim Fathers' heroic status in American history.

In 1588, the world's first sea atlas, *The Mariner's Mirrour*, by the Dutch sea pilot Lucas Janszoon Waghenaer, was published for the first time in English. The English edition, translated by Sir Anthony Ashley (one of the leaders of the expedition to Cádiz in which John Donne took part), includes a famous frontispiece by the Flemish-German engraver Theodor de Bry. The picture depicts human ingenuity in mastering the sea, with images of a range of nautical and map-making instruments, and two mariners, dressed like Shakespearean actors, holding lead-lines to gauge the depth of the sea. Above them, a group of people surround a blank globe looking excitedly and expectantly for the detail to be added. By comparison, the sea monsters at the bottom of the picture are relatively insignificant. This frontispiece speaks volumes of the changing western attitudes towards the sea during the age of discovery: fear and suspicion was giving way to optimism and a sense of opportunity. From a religious perspective, what was previously seen in negative terms – or at best as a place of spiritual testing – was now beginning to be seen more positively. The sea not only offered opportunities to access new resources, it also provided a new sense of purpose. Christian missionaries were prominent among those who filled in the blank globe on de Bry's frontispiece, and there was a place, too, for those escaping religious persecution.

There was, then, a strong religious dimension to the age of discovery. Not only did it provide missionaries and dissenters with the impetus to go to sea, it was the religious zeal of Columbus and others that led them to become explorers and sail into the unknown in the first place. Columbus may have been misplaced in thinking that he would bring about the end of the world, but what his voyages did instead was not only to inspire some of the great literary figures of the age, but help bring to an end a misplaced world-view or cosmology typified by T-O maps and driven by religious beliefs. It also created some of the most enduring and problematic geo-political issues of recent centuries, in which religion has been prominent. If this age of discovery had significant theological implications, so too did another which was about to begin.

1   Brian Fagan, *Fish on Friday: Feasting, Fasting and the Discovery of the New World* (New York: Basic Books, 2006), p. 145ff.
2   Djelal Kadir, *Columbus and the Ends of the Earth: Europe's Prophetic Rhetoric as Conquering Ideology* (Berkeley: University of California Press, 1992), p. 30.
3   Christopher Columbus (ed. Roberto Rusconi, tr. Blair Sullivan), *The Book of Prophecies edited by Christopher Columbus* (Berkeley and London: University of California Press, 1997), pp. 67-9.
4   *The Travels of Marco Polo the Venetian* (London: J.M. Dent, 1908), p. 324.
5   Pauline Moffitt Watts, 'Prophecy and Discovery: On the Spiritual Origins of Christopher Columbus's "Enterprise of the Indies"', *American Historical Review*, 90 (1985), p. 102.
6   Barry Cunliffe, *Facing the Ocean: The Atlantic and its Peoples 8000BC - AD1500* (Oxford: Oxford University Press, 2001), p.16.
7   Stephen Neill, *A History of Christian Missions*, second edition (London: Penguin, 1986). p. 150.
8   Steve Mentz, *At the Bottom of Shakespeare's Ocean* (London: Continuum, 2009), p. 3.
9   Dan Brayton, *Shakespeare's Ocean: An Ecocritical Exploration* (University of Virginia Press, 2012), p. 4.
10 Eucharistic Prayer G, *Common Worship: Services and Prayers for the Church of England* (London: Church House Publishing, 2000), p. 201.
11 A.F. Falconer, *Shakespeare and the Sea* (London: Constable, 1964), p. 147.
12 See Malcolm Guite, *Faith, Hope and Poetry: Theology and the Poetic Imagination* (Farnham: Ashgate, 2010), pp. 110-3.
13 Brigham Young University: John Donne Sermons, https://contentdm.lib.byu.edu/digital/

collection/JohnDonne/id/621, p.20.

14 Ibid., p. 21.

15 Brigham Young: https://contentdm.lib.byu.edu/digital/collection/JohnDonne/id/1236, p.1.

16 Ibid., pp. 2-3.

17 Ibid., pp. 17-8.

18 William Bradford, *History of Plymouth Plantation* (New York: Effingham, Maynard and Co., 1890), pp. 28-9.

6

The Book of Nature

I do not know what I may appear to the world,
but to myself I seem to have been only like a boy
playing on the sea-shore, and diverting myself
in now and then finding a smoother pebble or a
prettier shell than ordinary, whilst the great ocean
of truth lay all undiscovered before me.

Sir Isaac Newton

If territorial discoveries changed European mind-sets in the fifteenth
and early-sixteenth centuries, discoveries of another sort had a similar
impact two hundred years later. The late-seventeenth and early-eighteenth
centuries have been called the Age of Reason or Enlightenment, a period
in which reason and freedom were championed as values especially in
France, Germany, and Britain, and later in North America, and when the
'scientific method' of formulating and testing hypotheses through systematic
observation and experimentation came to the fore. If the age of discovery
changed our understanding of geography, the major scientific advances of the
Enlightenment fundamentally altered perceptions about the natural world.

While science and religion are often seen today as being in tension or
opposition, in the past they were often deeply interconnected, not least
during the Enlightenment when many leading scientists regarded their work
as an expression of their religious beliefs, or even as a form of worship. Those
who held such views included the towering figures of Sir Isaac Newton and
Robert Boyle, the founding father of chemistry. It was Boyle, writing in a
tract published in 1674, who summed-up this strongly held attitude towards
religion and science: 'the two great books, of nature and of scripture, have
the same author, so the study of the latter does not at all hinder an inquisitive
man's delight in the study of the former'.[1]

Boyle and his contemporaries were living at a time of transition for European Christianity. The emerging academic field of biblical criticism was beginning to produce scholars who challenged the long-held understanding of the factual accuracy of scripture, while organised religion and ecclesiastical authority were under attack as religious dissenters became more prominent. This period of religious flux, coinciding with rapid advances in science and the scientific way of thinking, provided fertile ground for the development of 'natural theology' – a method of seeking to understanding God through a combination of human reason and the study of the natural world. Natural theology was not a new concept. In Greek philosophy, the search for the 'first principle', or the ultimate source and origin of all things, is an early example of such an approach. Aristotle's *Physics*, dating from the fourth century BCE, includes his theory that the motion and change we witness and experience in creation derives from a 'first mover of all other movers' which is itself immovable. From this, Aristotle went on to equate the first mover with 'Mind'. Similarly, his near contemporary Plato argued for a cause of all being and all knowledge as the 'Good'. Their logic was similar to that of later theologians who similarly argued that all that exists derives from God.

The wisdom literature of Hebrew scripture provides examples of what might be described as the product of natural theology in ancient Jewish thought. This includes a passage from the Book of Job, when the good and pious Job questions why he is suffering, to which God replies out the whirlwind:

> Where were you when I laid the foundation of the earth?
> Tell me, if you have understanding.
> Who determined its measurements—surely you know!
>
> Or who shut in the sea with doors
> when it burst out from the womb?—
> when I made the clouds its garment,
> and thick darkness its swaddling band,
> and prescribed bounds for it,
> and set bars and doors,
> and said, 'Thus far shall you come, and no farther,
> and here shall your proud waves be stopped'?
>
> Have you entered into the springs of the sea,
> or walked in the recesses of the deep?
> Have the gates of death been revealed to you,

or have you seen the gates of deep darkness?
Have you comprehended the expanse of the earth?
Declare, if you know all this.

(Job 38:4-11, 16-18)

No wonder, then, that in the thirteenth century the Franciscan theologian St Bonaventure wrote of the natural world offering 'shadows, echoes, and pictures' of its Creator that are 'divinely given signs' of God's presence.[2]

What differentiated the approach to natural theology in the seventeenth and eighteenth centuries from its earlier forms was that its proponents sought to use the scientific study of the natural world to prove the existence of God. Thus natural theology became a tool for Christian apologetics – to defend Christianity against its objectors – rather than seeking to enhance our understanding of the nature of the Creator by carefully observing creation. This new take on natural theology was very much a product of the age of scientific discovery. The recently developed telescope and microscope were revealing patterns and structures at the cosmic and microscopic level. Laboratory experiments were providing evidence for the laws of nature, such as Boyle's Law concerning the relationship between the volume, pressure, and temperature of gases. Advances in mathematics were also providing a new language for explaining this natural order, and how different aspects of the natural world interacted and affected each other. It was as if the exploration of the natural world taking place at this time was revealing the dynamics of creation. What Newton and others discovered were apparently self-regulating systems, such as the motion of planets and comets, which could be expressed elegantly in mathematical formulae.

This new understanding of the natural order had two important theological consequences. First, it led to the rise of 'deism' – belief in God as a deity who set up the universe to run of its own accord. Boyle likened the universe to Strasbourg Cathedral's magnificent clock, an idea taken up and developed later by William Paley in his book *Natural Theology*, in which he famously likens God to a watchmaker, who has created a finely tuned and beautifully ordered, self-regulating world. This deistic view of God was in contrast to theism – the belief that God is somehow present and active in the world.

The other effect of scientific discovery on theology was to promote the argument for the existence of God 'by design'. Newton, Boyle, and others were observing the wonderful ordering of the natural world for the first time through the recent inventions of the telescope and microscope and seemed almost compelled to conclude that this provided overwhelming evidence for

the existence of an intelligent designer behind creation. The publication of
Robert Hooke's *Micrographia* in 1665 caused a sensation, providing the first
drawings of plants and insects as seen through a microscope. The magnificent
form even of a flea led Hooke to argue that the reason why the beauty of
natural objects increased when magnified was because 'he that was the
Author of all these things, was no other then [sic] Omnipotent; being able
to include as great a variety of parts and contrivances in the yet smallest
Discernable Point, as in those vaster bodies . . . such as the Earth, Sun, or
Planets.'[3] Hooke, like so many of his contemporaries, could not but link his
scientific observations to his Christian faith.

A natural system that came to be analysed theologically during the
Enlightenment was the hydrologic cycle. The concept of the re-circulation
of water between the sea and rivers dates back to antiquity, and appears in
Pliny the Younger's *Natural History* and Aristotle's *Meteorlogica*. The wisdom
literature of the Bible also hints at some sort of exchange between freshwater
and saltwater in Ecclesiastes 1:7:

> All streams run to the sea,
> but the sea is not full;
> to the place where the streams flow,
> there they continue to flow.

For centuries, the dominant view had been that water re-circulates between
the sea and rivers through subterranean passages. This view was challenged
and overturned in the eighteenth century following the publication, in 1681,
of a controversial book by the Cambridge theologian Thomas Burnet. The
first edition of Burnet's *Sacred Theory of the Earth* was in Latin. Three years
later it was republished in English as *Theory of the Earth*, and this new edition
proved to be both popular and provocative. Burnet was clearly influenced by
the argument from design, but this understanding of God and nature raised a
fundamental problem: how could the Earth be so physically imperfect if it was
created by a God who created a universe that was so well ordered? Burnet's
answer was that the Earth had been created perfect, and that 'deformities'
such as seas, valleys, and mountains were the consequence of God's response
to human sinfulness in bringing about the Flood, as described in the Book
of Genesis. In developing his argument, Burnet wanted to determine how
much water was required in the Flood to cover the Earth, and in doing so
subscribed to the subterranean view of the hydrologic cycle.

The publication of *Theory of the Earth* stimulated considerable interest
and discussion on two related topics: the hydrologic cycle and the biblical

Flood. Those influenced by the book included Newton who said of Burnet, 'Of our present sea, rocks, mountains etc., I think you have given the most plausible account.'[4] Others inspired by Burnet included Newton's protégé and successor as Lucasian Professor of Mathematics at Cambridge, William Whiston. Whiston's *A New Theory of the Earth,* published in 1696, was also concerned with the source of water for the Flood, but argued that as well as Burnet's subterranean waters, Halley's Comet left 'prodigious quantities' of water vapour on Earth. Linking the Flood to Halley's Comet enabled Whiston to give a precise date to when this happened: 28 November 2349 BCE. The philosopher John Locke said of Whiston that he 'explained so wonderful, and before Inexplicable Things in the great Changes of this Globe.'[5]

The debate over the Flood drew the attention of Edmond Halley himself, who gave two papers on the subject at the Royal Society in London in 1694. One of the issues Halley addressed was why the fossils of sea creatures were found on mountains, this being some time before the discovery of tectonic plates and an understanding about their role in forming mountains. Halley shared a widely held view that it was the result of the Flood, or an earlier flood, which he argued was caused by a comet or other astronomical body passing close by the Earth, the force of which resulted in:

> [a] great Agitation … in the Sea sufficient to answer for all those strange Appearances of heaping vast Quantities of Earth and high Cliffs upon Beds of Shells, which once were the Bottom of the Sea; and raising up Mountains where none were before.[6]

The explanation of geological processes in terms of the Flood came to be known as the 'diluvial theory'. Other influential thinkers who shared the view that fossils on mountains could be explained by the Flood included some of the pioneering figures in geology such as John Woodward, the Danish scientist Niels Stensen (known in English as Nicolas Steno), and the Swiss naturalist John Jakob Scheuchzer.

As well as the Flood, Burnet's work stimulated a debate on water circulation. One of Burnet's major critics was the Cambridge mathematician John Kiell, who argued that what Burnet called 'deformities' – the sea, valleys, and mountains – were, in fact, essential to sustain life through the hydrologic cycle. Kiell correctly described the hydrologic cycle not as the subterranean re-circulation of water, but as involving the evaporation of water from the sea to produce rain, which then waters the land, making it fertile. What became clear from the analysis by Kiell and others was that the size of the oceans was of crucial importance in determining the amount of rainfall, and therefore freshwater, available to make land fertile. As a result of this new understanding of the hydrologic cycle, the vast expanse of sea covering the Earth came to be seen as essential for sustaining life on land.

As the hydrologic cycle came to be better understood, so the oceans came to be seen as part of a well-ordered, life-giving system – a far cry from the ancient view of them as the dwelling place of the dead and the remnant of primordial chaos. This new understanding appealed to natural theologians, who were attracted by the beauty of this cyclical, self-perpetuating system and its life-sustaining properties. As the moral philosopher and philologist William Wollaston observed of the hydrologic cycle in *The Religion of Nature Delineated* (1722), 'I say, who can do this, and not see a *design*, in such regular pieces, so nicely wrought, and *so* preserved?'[7] As a result, natural theologians began to describe the sea positively, in terms of God's providence. One of the earliest to do so was the priest and naturalist John Ray:

> if there were but half the Sea that now is, there would be also but half the Quantity of Vapours, and consequently we could have but half so many Rivers as now there are to supply all the dry Land we have at present, and half as much more; for the Quantity of Vapours which are rais'd, bears a Proportion to the Surface whence they are rais'd, as well as to the Heat which rais'd them. The Wise Creator therefore did so prudently order it, that the Sea should be large enough to supply Vapours sufficient for all the Land, which it would not do if it were less than now it is.[8]

The sea's providential nature was seen not only in terms of watering the land, but also in providing humans with other useful resources. The theology was highly anthropocentric. As Ray also wrote:

> The Sea, what infinite Variety of Fishes doth it nourish! … How doth it constantly observe its Ebbs and Flows, its Spring and Nepe-Tides, and still retain its Saltness, so convenient for the Maintenance of its Inhabitants, serving also the Uses of Man for Navigation, and the Convenience of Carriage?[9]

The providential understanding of the hydrologic cycle was popularised by John Wesley who, in *A Survey of the Wisdom of God in Creation*, similarly asked rhetorically:

> Who has instructed the rivers to run in so many winding streams through vast tracts of land in order to water them so plentifully? Then

to disembogue themselves into the ocean, so making it the common centre for commerce: and thence to return through the earth and air, to their fountain heads, in one perpetual circulation?[10]

⌒

Just at the time when natural theology was proving highly influential, an event occurred that shook the faith of many and posed awkward questions to those promulgating the argument by design. At 9.30 a.m. on Sunday 1 November 1755 many of the Christian faithful in the Iberian Peninsula were at church celebrating All Saints Day when disaster struck in the form of an earthquake and tsunami. Lisbon was worst affected, where the death toll is estimated to be in the region of 10,000 to 15,000 including many killed by falling masonry inside churches. A British merchant who witnessed the disaster described how, after the earthquake, Lisbon was struck by the tsunami:

> a general Pannic was raised from a Crowd of People's [sic] running from the Water-side, all crying out the Sea was pouring in and would certainly overwhelm the City. This new Alarm, created such Horrors in the agitated Minds of the Populace, that vast Numbers of them ran screaming into the ruinated City again, where, a fresh Shock of the Earthquake immediately following, many of them were buried in the Ruins of falling Buildings.
>
> This Alarm was, however, not entirely without Foundation: For the Water of the River rose at once above twenty Feet perpendicular, and subsided again to its natural Pitch in less than a Minute's time. But the Horror and Distraction of the Multitude were so increased by this astonishing Phænomenon, that they appeared more shocking than even the very Operations of the Earthquake.[11]

The impact of the Lisbon earthquake was profound. As well as the deaths, injuries, and damage to buildings – including churches and 55 convents and monasteries – the event caused a theological crisis. For deists and theists alike, the earthquake and tsunami raised awkward questions. For deists, it posed the question, how could such natural disorder be reconciled with a God who had created a beautifully ordered universe? For theists, an immediate question was whether it was an act of divine judgment, and if so, for what?

The Lisbon earthquake and tsunami was not the first natural disaster to raise religious questions. One such event took place on 20 January 1607, when severe and rapid coastal flooding was experienced in the Bristol Channel, extending from Barnstaple in North Devon to Carmarthenshire in South

Wales up the Severn Estuary to Gloucester. The flooding, attributed to either a tsunami or a storm surge caused by a hurricane, led to a considerable loss of life. The exact death-toll is not known, but it is thought to have been in the thousands, with many animal fatalities as well as human – a point noted in an anonymous tract which was published after the event. *Gods Warning to his people of England* draws clear parallels between this flood and that in Genesis and concludes:

> This mercylesse Water breaking into the Bosome of the firme Land, hath proved a fearfull punishment, as well to all other living Creatures: as also to all Mankinde: Which if it had not been for the mercyfull promise of God, as the last dissolution of the World by Water, by the signe of the Rainbowe, which is still shewed us: we might have verily believed, this time had bin the very houre of Christ his coming: From which Element of Water, extended towardes us in this fearefull manner, good Lord deliver us all. Amen.[12]

While the Bristol Channel flood and similar events in the past had been interpreted as reprises of the Flood – divine punishment and warnings about human sinfulness – and/or portents of the end of the world, the rise of natural theology and deism in the interim meant that the Lisbon earthquake posed new theological issues. These were expressed by the French philosopher Voltaire in his 'Poem on the Lisbon Disaster or an Examination of the Axiom "All is well"':

> Unhappy mortals! Dark and mourning earth!
> Affrighted gathering of human kind!
> Eternal lingering of useless pain!
> Come ye philosophers, who cry 'All's well',
> And contemplate this ruin of a world
> Behold these shreds and cinders of your race,
> The child and mother heaped in common wreck,
> These scattered limbs beneath the marble shafts –
> A hundred thousand whom earth devours,
> Who, torn and bloody, palpitating yet,
> Entombed beneath their hospitable roofs,
> In racking torment end their stricken lives!
> To those expiring murmurs of distress,
> To that appalling spectacle of woe,
> Will ye reply 'You do but illustrate

The iron laws that chain the will of God'?
Say ye, o'er that yet quivering mass of flesh:
'God is avenged: the wage of sin is death'?
What crime, what sin, had those young hearts conceived
That lie, bleeding and torn, on mother's breast?
Did fallen Lisbon deeper drink of vice
Than London, Paris, or sunlit Madrid?
In these men dance; at Lisbon yawns the abyss.
Tranquil spectators of your brothers' wreck,
Unmoved by this repellent dance of death,
Who calmly seek the reason of such storms,
Let them but lash your own security;
Your tears will mingle freely with the flood.[13]

For the deist Voltaire, God was ultimately responsible for the suffering, not because God willed it to happen but simply because God is the source of all life and being but has no involvement in our affairs. Voltaire's deism was therefore bleak and pessimistic, in contrast to that of his fellow countryman Rousseau who attributed the disaster not to God but to human folly – that it is not 'nature's way' for people to live in crowded cities, and had they not done so then the destruction would have been far less severe. As Rousseau responded to Voltaire, 'I see not where we must look for the source of moral evil except in man, a free, improved, and yet corrupt being; and as to physical evils … they must be unavoidable in every system of which man constitutes a part.'[14]

Despite the questions raised by the Lisbon earthquake, the proof of God from design remained influential into the nineteenth century. William Paley's *Natural Theology*, published in 1802, sets out the argument in its classic form and became a best-seller. Paley provides a wide range of examples of beautifully ordered natural systems drawn from anatomy and botany. He compares the eye with a telescope, regards the human neck as 'the most complicated, or the most flexible, machine, that was ever contrived',[15] and describes the providential nature of grasses which are 'Nature's care': 'Cattle feed upon their leaves; birds upon their smaller seeds; men upon the larger; for few readers need to be told that the plants, which produce our bread corn, belong to this class.'[16] What Paley offered is not 'proof' in the sense of concrete evidence for God's existence, but an appeal to probability by providing example after example of the wonders of nature aimed at convincing the reader that, collectively, they point to an intelligent designer. Paley concludes,

'The marks of *design* are too strong to be gotten over. Design must have a designer. That designer must have been a person. That person is God.'[17]

A similar 'weight of evidence' approach was taken by William Buckland, the brilliant and eccentric Canon of Christ Church, Oxford and Dean of Westminster, who, as well as attempting to eat his way through the animal kingdom (his favourite meal was supposedly mice on toast) and keeping a pet bear and hyena, was one of the founders of modern geology. In *Geology and Mineralogy, considered with reference to Natural Theology*, published in 1836, Buckland sought to 'supply a chain of connected evidence, amounting to demonstration, of the continuous Being, and of many of the highest Attributes of the One Living and True God.'[18] This evidence included the hydrologic cycle, of which Buckland commented:

> As the presence of water is essential both to animal and vegetable existence, the adjustment of the Earth's surface to supply this necessary fluid, in due proportion to the demand, affords one of the many proofs of Design.[19]

While the Lisbon earthquake posed awkward theological questions in the eighteenth century, in the nineteenth century theology was presented with a new challenge, and one which fundamentally changed the way we think about the natural world – not least the ideas posited by Paley and Buckland. The challenge came from Charles Darwin's observations during his five years on board the survey ship the *Beagle* in the 1830s. The voyage provided the information that led to Darwin's evolutionary theory, as set out in *On the Origin of Species by Means of Natural Selection*, published in 1859. Controversial as Darwin's theory was – and to some extent still is – it effectively pulled the rug from under the feet of those who argued that the natural order was divinely ordained in the sense that God had created a beautifully balanced world, with fixed species, for the benefit of humanity.

The idea of evolutionary development was not new. In Book V of *On the Literal Interpretation of Genesis*, Augustine of Hippo put forward as early as 415 the idea the creatures, having been created by God, gradually assume their present form. Darwinism, however, was different from Augustine's theistic evolution. Rather than evolving in a way pre-ordained by God, Darwinian evolution involved competition and the 'survival of the fittest'. Not only did this challenge the widely held view of fixed species, but the idea of an intelligent designer. Darwinism was in stark contrast to the concept of the dynamics of creation as described by Paley, Buckland, and others. Theology needed to be reconciled to the developmental understanding of the natural world, and in particular to the concepts of evolution and natural selection.

The work of Darwin and other evolutionists was as much a turning point for theology as it was for science, and for some it led to a crisis of faith. One person deeply affected by the changing scientific understanding of the natural world was the prominent Victorian scientist and populariser of science, Philip Henry Gosse. The intellectual and spiritual turmoil Gosse faced was described by his son, Edmund Gosse, in his powerful autobiographical study of family relationships, *Father and Son: A Study of Two Temperaments*. Gosse senior was a self-taught naturalist and marine biologist, and held in sufficient esteem by his scientific peers for his research and publications such as *A Manual of Marine Zoology* to be elected as a Fellow of the Royal Society in 1856. Gosse is also credited with popularizing, and giving name to, the aquarium. He used tanks of seawater to recreate the ecology of rock pools for research purposes, and his popular book *A Handbook to the Marine Aquarium* helped create something of a craze for aquariums in mid-Victorian homes.

As well as being fascinated by the natural world, and especially the marine environment, Gosse was also deeply religious. As a young man, while living in Newfoundland, Gosse had a powerful conversion experience and initially found a home among Methodists. After returning to England, Gosse then became a member of the Brethren – or Plymouth Brethren – a conservative dissenting evangelical movement, which places supreme authority in the Bible, a faith he shared with his wife, Emily. Gosse's fascination in the natural world quickly became a Christian vocation. He believed that the wonderfully-balanced eco-systems that he observed in rock pools and was able to recreate through careful analysis in aquariums were evidence of an intelligent designer, and he was keen to relate this through his writings.

In *Father and Son*, Edmund Gosse portrays his father as stern and as a severe religious fanatic. This view has been challenged by the biographer of both Gosses, Ann Thwaite, who regards Edmund Gosse as an unreliable witness, suggesting that his father was in reality a much kinder and more attractive person than his son described. What is not in dispute, however, is that Philip Henry Gosse was strongly, and conservatively, religious. In *Father and Son*, Edmund Gosse says of his parents' attitude to the Bible:

> For [my mother] and for my Father, nothing was symbolic, nothing allegorical or allusive in any part of Scripture, except what was, in so many words, proffered as a parable or a picture ... Both my parents, I think, were devoid of sympathetic imagination; in my Father, I am

sure, it was singularly absent. Hence, although their faith was strenuous, that many persons may have called it fanatical, there was no mysticism about them. They were rather the opposite extreme, to the cultivation of a rigid and iconoclastic literalness.'[20]

With such a rigid mind-set, it is understandable that Philip Henry Gosse became deeply troubled by the rise of the developmental understanding of nature. Aware that the geologist Sir Charles Lyell was planning to publish a book on the developmental nature of geology, Gosse decided to publish a counter-argument justifying the long-held belief that species had been created by God as fixed kinds, as described in the opening passages of Genesis. Gosse's theory was set out in his 1857 book *Omphalos*, the Greek word for navel. The thrust of his argument was that just as the first man, Adam, would certainly have been created in a sudden act of creation with a navel (despite not having been born of a mother, and therefore not attached to an umbilical cord), so too was the Earth created suddenly with only the appearance of life having previously existed, such as the presence of fossils. It was Gosse's belief that his theory reconciled scripture with the book of nature. However, *Omphalos* – which was republished as *Creation* – was badly received. As Edmund Gosse recalled:

> In the course of that dismal winter, as the post began to bring in private letters, few and chilly, and public reviews, many and scornful, my Father looked in vain for the approval of the churches, and in vain for the acquiescence of the scientific societies, and in vain for the gratitude of those 'thousands of thinking persons', which he had rashly assured himself of receiving. As his reconciliation of Scripture statements and geological deductions was welcomed nowhere, as Darwin continued silent, and the youthful Huxley was scornful, and even Charles Kingsley, from whom my Father had expected the most instant appreciation, wrote that he could not 'give up the painful and slow conclusion of five and twenty years' study of geology, and believe that God has written on the rocks one enormous and superfluous lie', – as all this happened or failed to happen, a gloom, cold and dismal, descended upon our morning teacups. It was what the poets mean by an 'inspissated' gloom; it thickened day by day, as hope and self-confidence evaporated in thin clouds of disappointment. My Father was not prepared for such a fate. He had been the spoiled darling of the public, the constant favourite of the press, and now, like the dark angels of old,

so huge a rout
Encumbered him with ruin.

He could not recover from amazement at having offended everybody
by an enterprise which had been undertaken in the cause of universal
reconciliation.[21]

The publication of *Omphalos* in 1857 and *The Origin of Species* two years later
marks a turning point in our understanding of the natural world. Gosse and
Darwin, who knew and admired each other, stand in contrast: Gosse, the
religious dissenter, steeped in a way of thinking encouraged by generations
of religiously motivated scientists, was symbolic of a rapidly-vanishing
intellectual world-view. Darwin, who went to Cambridge University with
the intention of becoming ordained in the Church of England, stood for
something different. Darwin never expressed atheistic views, but was
certainly critical of reading the Bible – particularly the creation narratives
– as history.

Just as Darwin's ideas changed science, so too did they have a profound
effect on theology. Philip Henry Gosse had looked at the natural world
with wonder, as well as with the forensic eye of a scientist who saw in it
the work of an intelligent designer. As Gosse's approach to natural theology
lost credibility, so a new approach emerged, this time associated with the
discipline of psychology. No longer was the focus on proving God's existence
by appealing to the beauty and elegance of creation, but on how the natural
world could instil in people a sense of God's presence. In some respects, this
new form of natural theology had emerged not so much from the world of
science but the arts, and its origins can be traced back several centuries and
to people who, like Gosse, were drawn powerfully to the sea.

1 Robert Boyle, *The Excellency of Theology Compar'd with Natural Philosophy* (London, 1674), p. 121.
2 Philotheus Boehner and Zachary Hayes (eds.) *Works of St Bonaventure*, vol. 2, *Itinerarium Mentis in Deum* (New York: Franciscan Institute Publications, 2002), p. 77.
3 Robert Hooke, *Micrographia: or Some Physiological Descriptions of Minute Bodies made by Magnifying Glasses with Observations and Inquiries Thereupon* (London, 1665), p. 2.
4 H.S. Thayer (ed.), *Newton's Philosophy of Nature: Selections from His Writings* (New York: Dover, 2005), p. 58.
5 *The Works of John Locke*, vol. 3 (London: Awnsham Churchill, 1722), p. 556.

6   Edmond Halley, *Some Considerations about the Cause of the Universal Deluge, laid before the Royal Society on the 12th of Dec. 1694*, p. 118.

7   William Wollaston, *The Religion of Nature Delineated* (London, 1725), p. 82.

8   John Ray, *The Wisdom of God Manifested in the Works of Creation*, First Part (London, 1735), p. 80.

9   Ibid., pp. 78-9.

10 John Wesley, *A Survey of the Wisdom of God in the Creation: or A Compendium of Natural Philosophy*, vol. 2 (New York: Methodist Episcopal Church, 1823), p. 181.

11 Thomas Hunter, *A Historical Account of Earthquakes, Extracted from the most Authentick Historians* (Liverpool, 1756), p. 59.

12 Anon., *Gods Warning to his people of England* (London, 1607), pp. 14-5.

13 Voltaire (trans. J. McCabe), *Toleration and Other Essays* (New York and London: G.P. Putnam's sons, 1912), pp. 255-6.

14 *The Works of J.J. Rousseau*, vol. 9 (Edinburgh: John Donaldson, 1774), p. 318.

15 William Paley, *Natural Theology* (New York: American Tract Society, 1886), p. 68.

16 Ibid., p. 236.

17 Ibid., p. 285.

18 William Buckland, *Geology and Mineralogy Considered with Reference to Natural Theology*, vol. 1 (London: William Pickering, 1836), p. viii.

19 Ibid., p. 556.

20 Edmund Gosse *Father and Son: A Study of Two Temperaments* (London: William Heinemann, 1907), p. 75.

21 Ibid., pp. 122-3.

7

The Sea of Faith

If there is poetry in my book about the sea, it is not because I deliberately put it there, but because no one could write truthfully about the sea and leave out the poetry.

Rachel Carson

While natural theology was making theologians out of scientists – and creating new theological controversies – it was also helping to create a new awareness of nature which had wider implications beyond the world of science, and more akin to the earlier concept of natural theology in which the natural world 'speaks' of the divine. Religious feelings related to awe and wonder were not limited to the findings of science, but were also associated with changing perceptions of landscapes. A trigger for this was the writings of several well-known travellers, including the dramatist John Dennis and the third Earl of Shaftesbury, and their descriptions of crossing the Alps. Mountains in particular seem to have initially rekindled an awareness of the ancient concept of 'the sublime'.

In 1756, the philosopher and politician Edmund Burke published what proved to be a highly influential tract. In *A Philosophical Enquiry into the Origin of Our Ideas of the Sublime and Beautiful*, Burke made a contrast between what is beautiful and what is sublime. Beauty, he argued, stems from what is aesthetically pleasing and well formed. The sublime, however, does not involve beauty but instead evokes strong feelings of awe and is particularly associated with those things that incite fear. For Burke, the key to the sublime is terror, and, as he put it, while mountains can terrify, 'the ocean is an object of no small terror'.[1] Burke also argued that 'greatness of dimension' and a sense of infinity are sources of the sublime. While the sea is not infinite, as he points out, 'There are scarce any things which can become the objects of our senses, that are really and in their own nature infinite. But the eye not being able to perceive the bounds of many things, they seem to be infinite, and they produce the same effects as if they were really so.'[2] Burke was influenced by Burnet's *Sacred Theory of the Earth*, in which, as well as analysing the natural world from a theological perspective, its author described how it affected him spiritually:

> The greatest objects of Nature are, methinks, the most pleasing to behold; and next to the great Concave of the Heavens, and those boundless Regions where the Stars inhabit, there is nothing that I look upon with more pleasure than the wide Sea and the Mountains of the Earth. There is something august and stately in the Air of these things, that inspires the mind with great thoughts and passions; We do naturally, upon such occasions, think of God and his greatness; and whatsoever hath but the shadow and appearance of the INFINITE, as all things have that are too big for our comprehension, they fill and over-bear the mind with their Excess, and cast it into a pleasing kind of stupor and admiration.[3]

Another in Burke's circle was the writer and politician Joseph Addison, who wrote the hymn 'The spacious firmament on high'. Like Burnet, Addison also found the sea could evoke deep religious feelings:

> of all objects that I have ever seen, there is none which affects my imagination so much as the sea or ocean. I cannot see the heavings of this prodigious bulk of waters, even in a calm, without a very pleasing astonishment; but when it is worked up in a tempest, so that the horizon on every side is nothing but foaming billows and floating mountains, it is impossible to describe the agreeable horror that rises from such a prospect... I must confess, it is impossible for me to survey this world of fluid matter, without thinking on the hand that first poured it out, and made a proper channel for its reception. Such an object naturally raises in my thoughts the idea of an Almighty Being, and convinces me of his existence as much as metaphysical demonstration. The imagination prompts the understanding, and, by the greatness of the sensible object, produces in it the idea of a Being who is neither circumscribed by time nor space.[4]

Burke's tract explored what he was observing in society, and what others like Burnet and Addison were describing: the allure of wild landscapes – and seascapes – things that in the past were not only considered dangerous but also deeply unattractive. Burke was aware of changing perceptions: he was witnessing the birth of Romanticism.

Romanticism was, in the words of Marilyn Butler, a 'posthumous movement'.[5] The 'Romantics' of the late-eighteenth and early-nineteenth centuries had no inclination they would be grouped together and given such an epithet, as the term was not used until the 1860s. What the term 'Romanticism' describes is, in essence, a social and artistic response to changes taking place in European society in the eighteenth century. With its emphasis on feelings, the imagination, and the sublime aspects of the natural world, Romanticism was in sharp contrast to the Enlightenment's championing of rational thought and pursuit of beauty through carefully proportioned Neo-Classical art. Romanticism was, perhaps, more than anything else an antidote to the rapid emergence of materialism and the exploitation of the natural world associated with industrialisation and urbanisation – an alternative, counter-balancing response to the spirit of the age. At one level Romanticism was an aesthetic movement expressed primarily through the arts. At another, it was an expression of self-discovery, almost akin to a religious quest – and for some it was both. Among the self- or soul-searching and artistry, Romantics were drawn to the sea and the sea-shore, which provided an environment that was highly conducive to introspection and the search for self-knowledge – something acknowledged from at least the time when those drawn to the monastic life sought 'a desert in the ocean'. Romantics actively sought similar intense feelings. As Alain Corbin observes in his study of the seaside, the expanse of a sea-shore 'furthers the longing for pantheistic merging, the desire to become one with the universe that plagued the Romantics'.[6]

While it is hard to pin down a precise definition of Romanticism it has a number of key features, many of which were fed by the experience of being on, or by, the sea. Romanticism spurned change: the sea, more than anything else, speaks of changelessness. Romanticism harked back to antiquity and beyond: it would be hard, if not impossible, to differentiate looking out to sea today from doing the same thousands of years ago. As Corbin has noted, Romantics were drawn to the concept of the sea (as expressed in the opening of Genesis) as 'the substance that preceded all creation and all form'.[7] Romanticism was sensual: the experience of walking on a beach, breathing the sea air, feeling the wind and sand, listening to the sound of waves and sea birds, and absorbing the smells is a heightened sensory experience, as is plunging into the sea. Romanticism was about escaping what were seen as forces gripping society: the sea speaks of freedom. Romanticism held a fascination with awe: the vastness and power of the sea is awe-inspiring. Romanticism drew on melancholia and had a fascination with death. The stark emptiness of a seascape can induce such feelings, and at the time of the rise of Romanticism death at sea was common. It is not surprising therefore that the sea was the muse for some of the most influential figures in the Romantic Movement.

Perhaps more than any other British painter, J. M. W. Turner had the ability to express the sublime, to which he was greatly attracted. He was particularly drawn to the violence of nature, and found inspiration from the power of the sea, a subject to which he frequently turned and which proved fertile territory for his genius in working with light. The sea clearly gripped Turner at an early age. His first exhibited oil painting, *Fishermen at Sea*, was painted in 1796 when he was sixteen. Turner claimed to have gone to extraordinary lengths to paint one of his greatest works, *Snowstorm –Steamboat off a Harbour's Mouth*, which was first exhibited in 1842 when the painter was 67. According to Turner, 'I got the sailors to lash me to the mast to observe it; I was lashed for four hours, and I did not expect to escape, but I felt bound to record it if I did.'[8] While the veracity of this story is highly questionable, it is likely – in true Romantic fashion – that Turner was casting himself as a latter-day Odysseus.

Turner's contemporary, the German artist Caspar David Friedrich, made the spiritual dimension of Romanticism explicit in many of his works. One of his most famous paintings, *Monk by the Sea* (which appears on the cover of this book), depicts a tiny figure standing on a sand dune looking out towards a rough, green sea and a vast, grey sky. The art historian Robert Rosenblum described the painting as expressing 'the mystic trinity of sky, water and earth' that 'appears to emanate from one unseen source.'[9] The painting was criticised when first exhibited for not having a *repoussier*, an image in the foreground that draws the viewer's eye into the depth of the picture. However, it is the absence of such a device that makes the picture so powerful. The viewer's eye is drawn immediately to the background of sky and sea before noticing the tiny monk in the foreground, which, in Rosenblum's words, creates 'a poignant contrast between the infinite vastness of a pantheistic God and the infinite smallness of His creatures.'[10]

While the sea influenced the visual arts, it is in the poetry of the Romantic Movement that its presence is most evident. All the great Romantic poets found inspiration from the sea or sea-shore. In 'On the Sea', John Keats contrasts the experience of being on a desolate shore with urban life:

Oh, ye! who have your eyeballs vexed and tired,
Feast them upon the wideness of the Sea;
Oh ye! whose ears are dinned with uproar rude,
Or fed too much with cloying melody –
Sit ye near some old Cavern's Mouth and brood,
Until ye start, as if the sea nymphs quired!

For William Wordsworth, being 'By the Sea' in Calais in 1802 with his nine year-old daughter, Caroline Vallon, stirred distinctly religious feelings:

It is a beauteous evening, calm and free;
The holy time is quiet as a nun
Breathless with adoration; the broad sun
Is sinking down in its tranquillity;
The gentleness of heaven is on the sea:
Listen! the mighty Being is awake,
And doth with his eternal motion make
A sound like thunder –everlastingly.
Dear child! dear girl! that walkest with me here,
If thou appear untouched by solemn thought
Thy nature is not therefore less divine:
Thou liest in Abraham's bosom all the year,
And worshipp'st at the Temple's inner shrine,
God being with thee when we know it not.

Although an atheist, Percy Bysshe Shelley's poem 'Love's Philosophy' draws on the Neo-Platonic image of merging waters to describe unity in nature in almost religious terms, and then uses it to express the unity of an intimate human relationship:

The fountains mingle with the river
And the rivers with the ocean,
The winds of heaven mix for ever
With a sweet emotion,
Nothing in the world is single;
All things by a law divine
In one spirit meet and mingle.
Why not I with thine?—

See the mountains kiss high heaven
And the waves clasp one another;

> No sister-flower would be forgiven
> If it disdained its brother;
> And the sunlight clasps the earth
> And the moonbeams kiss the sea:
> What is all this sweet work worth
> If thou kiss not me?

In stark contrast, Shelley's deliberately unfinished 'A Vision of the Sea' explores humanity's experience of terrifying natural forces, in this case a storm at sea which causes a ship-wreck:

> 'Tis the terror of tempest. The rags of the sail
> Are flickering in ribbons within the fierce gale:
> From the stark night of vapours the dim rain is driven …

Written in Pisa in 1820, the poem proved sadly prophetic. Two years later, while sailing in his newly-acquired boat the *Don Juan*, Shelley was caught in a sudden storm in the Gulf of Spezia on the west coast of Italy, and drowned. Shelley had modified the *Don Juan* – and in the process made her unstable – in order to make it faster than the *Bolivar*, the boat of his fellow-poet, Lord Byron. In fact, the original plan was for the *Bolivar* to sail alongside the *Don Juan* on its fateful journey.

Shelley, who could not swim, could spend hours gazing into the sea. Byron, in contrast, preferred the visceral experience of being in water (he once swam the Hellespont – the 38 mile strait that connects the Sea of Marmara and the Aegean). 'I can keep myself up for hours in the sea', said Byron, 'I delight in it, and come out with a buoyancy of spirits I never feel on any other occasion.'[11] This delight is apparent the work that made Byron famous, the narrative poem *Childe Harold's Pilgrimage*. Published in four parts, or cantos, between 1812 and 1818, the poem describes a young British nobleman's search for meaning in a corrupted and sinful world as he travels from country to country. The poem is almost certainly semi-autobiographical (although Byron denied it), drawing on his experiences of touring Europe from 1809 to 1811 after finishing his studies at Trinity College, Cambridge. The poem begins with a voyage, and returns on several occasions to consider the sea. In Canto 2, Byron describes how looking into the sea can change one's perspective and make one reflective:

> Thus bending o'er the vessel's laving side,
> To gaze on Dian's wave-reflected sphere,

The soul forgets her schemes of Hope and Pride,
And flies unconscious o'er each backward year.

In Canto 3, Byron expresses what an experience of the sublime can evoke: a sense of connectedness with something much greater than oneself: 'Are not the mountains, waves, and skies a part / Of me and of my soul, as I of them?', something he describes in greater depth near the end of the poem:

> There is a pleasure in the pathless woods,
> There is a rapture on the lonely shore,
> There is society where none intrudes,
> By the deep Sea, and music in its roar:
> I love not Man the less, but Nature more,
> From these our interviews, in which I steal
> From all I may be, or have been before,
> To mingle with the Universe, and feel
> What I can ne'er express, yet cannot all conceal.

The poem's conclusion is both deeply religious and an expression of Byron's love for the sea:

> Thou glorious mirror, where the Almighty's form
> Glasses itself in tempests; in all time,
> Calm or convulsed—in breeze, or gale, or storm,
> Icing the pole, or in the torrid clime
> Dark-heaving;—boundless, endless, and sublime—
> The image of Eternity—the throne
> Of the Invisible; even from out thy slime
> The monsters of the deep are made; each zone
> Obeys thee: thou goest forth, dread, fathomless, alone.
>
> And I have loved thee, Ocean! and my joy
> Of youthful sports was on thy breast to be
> Borne like thy bubbles, onward: from a boy
> I wantoned with thy breakers—they to me
> Were a delight; and if the freshening sea
> Made them a terror – 'twas a pleasing fear,
> For I was as it were a child of thee,
> And trusted to thy billows far and near,
> And laid my hand upon thy mane – as I do here.

The sea is, of course, central to another epic Romantic poem: Samuel Taylor Coleridge's *The Rime of the Ancient Mariner*. The poem is so evocative of a sea voyage that it is hard to imagine that at the time of writing Coleridge had never set foot off land. He was, however, familiar with the port of Bristol and an avid reader of books about travel and adventure. Most important of all, though, he was familiar with the Bristol Channel. For three years from 1796 Coleridge lived near the North Somerset coast at Nether Stowey. Often accompanied by his friends, fellow poet William Wordsworth and his sister Dorothy, Coleridge would go for long coastal walks across the Quantocks and Exmoor, so much so that there is now a designated 51 mile 'Coleridge Way' from Nether Stowey to Lynton and Lynmouth. Dorothy Wordsworth's journal gives a flavour of what they experienced:

> Walked with Coleridge over the hills. The sea at first obscured by vapour; that vapour afterwards slid in one mighty mass along the sea-shore; the islands and one point of land clear beyond it. The distant country (which was purple in the clear dull air), overhung by straggling clouds that sailed over it, appeared like the darker clouds, which are often seen at a great distance apparently, motionless, while the nearer ones pass quickly over them, driven by the lower winds. I never saw such a union of earth, sky, and sea.[12]

It was on one such walk in November 1797 that Coleridge and William Wordsworth decided to collaborate on a sea-based poem, clearly inspired by the locality, including the 'wood, which slopes down to the sea' and the harbour at Watchet, where they stayed overnight. Eventually, *The Rime of the Ancient Mariner* was written by Coleridge alone, with an acknowledgement to Wordsworth in the introduction.

Coleridge had a deep interest in theology, and at its heart the *Rime* is a theological work: a Christian allegory of navigating the ups-and-downs of life. The poem describes a long voyage which begins well, and then disaster strikes. The turning point is when, for no good reason, the mariner kills an albatross that had been accompanying his ship. This wanton killing proves to be the harbinger of a series of horrific experiences. With all the crew except the mariner dead, eventually – and apparently by God's grace – the ship returns from its voyage. Curiously, as the poet Malcolm Guite points out, Coleridge's own troubled life went on to mirror the experience of the ancient mariner.[13] For Coleridge, disaster struck in the form of opium addiction. Coleridge suffered bouts of ill health, both physical and mental, the breakdown of his marriage, and a troubled relationship with the woman he loved. It was only in later life, after he went to live with a doctor, James Gillman, who helped him handle his addiction, that Coleridge regained a degree of stability with a return of some of his early genius. As Guite also shows, while personally prescient for Coleridge, *The Rime of the Ancient Mariner* was also his stinging theological critique of Enlightenment thinking. Influenced by Neo-Platonism, Coleridge had a strong belief that nature has a sacred quality, providing a symbolic language that speaks of the divine and offering, to those open to such symbols, a gateway to God. As Coleridge later put it in his theological work, *The Statesman Manual*, 'a Symbol … is characterized by … the translucence of the Eternal through and in the Temporal.'[14]

Coleridge's spiritual understanding of nature could hardly be more different to the highly mechanistic Enlightenment view, which, from a religious perspective, saw the natural world as the creation of a deity who was a 'watchmaker'. Wonderful as the natural world was, it was essentially a complex machine activated and left to run by a remote God. Such a mechanistic understanding of the world helped create a mind-set that saw nature in instrumental terms, with no intrinsic value in itself, making the natural world ripe for human exploitation – as indeed was the case with the industrial revolution. Coleridge found the Enlightenment world-view deadening, and attacked it in his poem. By killing the albatross for no good reason, the ancient mariner represents the mechanistic, instrumental mind-set that Coleridge abhorred. To Coleridge, the consequence of such an attitude to the natural world could be disastrous, and only redeemable by God's grace.

The *Rime* also includes a verse in which the mariner is in the depths of despair:

> Alone, alone, all, all alone,
> Alone on a wide wide sea!
> And never a Saint had pity on
> My soul in agony.

While for Coleridge this was a temporary state on the mariner's journey of faith, melancholy and a profound sense of loneliness – the absence of God – is a real condition experienced by many people of faith, sometimes leading to a loss of faith. This is something also expressed in some of the great Romantic poetry of the nineteenth century. In his poem 'The Stream of Life', Arthur Hugh Clough, who had personal struggles with Christianity, described life as a 'stream descending to the sea' of death:

O end to which our currents tend,
Inevitable sea,
To which we flow, what do we know,
What shall we guess of thee?

A roar we hear upon thy shore,
As we our course fulfil;
Scarce we divine a sun will shine
And be above us still.

For Matthew Arnold, who also grappled with religion, the receding tide 'On Dover Beach' provided a powerful metaphor for the decline of Christianity he witnessed in the mid-nineteenth century:

The Sea of Faith
Was once, too, at the full, and round earth's shore
Lay like the folds of a bright girdle furled.
But now I only hear
Its melancholy, long, withdrawing roar,
Retreating, to the breath
Of the night-wind, down the vast edges drear
And naked shingles of the world.

～

The Romantic poets included people of deep – if unorthodox – faith, such as Coleridge, as well as atheists, such as Shelley. What they shared in common, though, was a profound sense of connectedness with nature. For some, this spoke of a Creator, for others it spoke of itself – nature. In the opening of his book *The God Delusion*, the strident atheist biologist Richard Dawkins ponders why an intense fascination with nature led his former school chaplain towards God and him in the other direction.[15] This twenty-first century personal conundrum in many ways echoes what happened in society at large the eighteenth and nineteenth centuries. While the Enlightenment encouraged a scientific, literalist way of thinking about the world, Romanticism stimulated an alternative, imaginative approach.

The psychiatrist and philosopher Iain McGilchrist explores the relationship between the Enlightenment and Romanticism in his book *The Master and his Emissary: The Divided Brain and the Making of the Western World*. McGilchrist's starting point is how the human brain functions, and he goes on to consider its wider implications. His argument, based on a vast body of neurological research, is that while the simplified view that the left hemisphere of the brain deals with reason and the right with imagination is false, there is nevertheless a profound difference between the two hemispheres.

Reason and imagination, McGilchrist argues, involve both sides of the brain working together. The left hemisphere, however, deals with narrow, sharply-focused attention to detail. The right hemisphere gives us a sustained, broad, open, vigilant alertness to the world around us. The left hemisphere majors on language; the right gives us the capacity for metaphor, to understand body language, and the symbolic. Crucially, both hemispheres are aided by the frontal lobe, the function of which is to inhibit the rest of the brain. Other animals do not have this mental brake pedal – they live for the moment. In contrast, the human frontal lobe enables us to stand back in time and space and distance ourselves from the world. With this mental detachment, we develop the capacity to think deeply and reflect and apply our minds to manipulate the world; and it also gives us the capacity to empathise with others.

From this starting point, McGilchrist argues that cultures are shaped by the cumulative effect of the way we think, and that over time western culture has changed significantly in relation to brain function. Looking back to classical times – the era of the Greek philosophers – and others, McGilchrist sees a wonderful balance between the right and the left hemispheres. Over time, however, he argues that that western cultures have evolved, or been conditioned, to be dominated by the left hemisphere. The reason for this is that the left hemisphere has an advantage over the right: it enables us to talk convincingly about the things that the left hemisphere majors on, and so it has a competitive edge over the right. In this way, McGilchrist sees the Enlightenment as a period of left-hemisphere dominance, with its 'pursuit of certainty and clarity', and Romanticism as a response to address this imbalance.[16]

If McGilchrist is right, then as well as perhaps helping to explain Dawkins' conundrum, he also helps us to understand something fundamental to what this book seeks to explore. On the one hand, the dangerous, capricious sea – the remnant of primordial chaos – demands not only our respect, but also our focused attention to understand its ways to be useful for our purposes, such as travel and fishing. On the other hand, the sea provides a rich source of inspiration for the imagination, as clearly demonstrated by the Romantic poets.

It is all too easy to over-romanticise the Romantic poets. As well as creating works of art many of them were also seeking to make a living through their publications, responding to the needs of their publishers and audience – and judging by their popularity, poems about the sea were in demand. The popularity of sea poetry is indicative of a broader, public attraction to the sea, and it is no coincidence that Romanticism coincided with the growth of the seaside holiday.

The origin of seaside tourism – at least in Britain – owes much to the association of water with healing. In the medieval period, it was common throughout Europe for freshwater springs, often called wells, to be venerated and associated with healing conducted by local saints. One such is St Frideswide, patron saint of Oxford, who is associated with a well with healing properties in the nearby village of Binsey. It is estimated that that there are over 8,000 holy wells in the British Isles in places including Wells in Somerset and Holywell in Flintshire. By the mid-sixteenth century, the emerging medical profession drew on the tradition of healing springs by prescribing bathing in, and drinking, natural mineral water for a wide range of illnesses. The supposed medicinal properties of water led to the development of spas such as at Bath and Buxton. Then, in the mid-eighteenth century, attention turned from mineral water to sea water. This development owed much to the popularity of Dr Richard Russell's *Dissertation on the Use of Sea Water in the Diseases of the Glands*, which was published in 1750. This book helped promote Scarborough, Brighton, Margate, and several South Devon seaside towns as health resorts. This development coincided with Britain's rapidly growing urban population seeking respite and relaxation away from polluted and crowded towns and cities, and these health and other resorts started to attract large numbers of people who wanted to sea-bathe purely for pleasure. Soon the seaside became a favourite destination and a new leisure industry was born, and one which expanded rapidly in the mid-nineteenth century with the advent of the railway.

As Adam Nicolson has pointed out, the prevailing European view of beaches before the eighteenth century was that they 'smelled disgusting' and were 'stiff with rot'.[17] Within decades, however, thousands of people were flocking to the seaside to breathe its healthy air. Similarly, just as Romanticism is associated with changing perceptions of the natural world through the appreciation of the sublime, the sociologist John Urry has argued that the eighteenth century witnessed the emergence of the 'tourist gaze', by which people began to look at the world around them as a means of enjoyment, and in order to disconnect themselves from their normal day-to-day lives. One

example of the impact of the tourist gaze is that before the advent of seaside ·
resorts it was normal for houses on the coast to face inland, but tourism
made sea-views attractive and sought after.[18] There may be another factor at
play, however. Psychological research shows that aquatic environments, or
'blue space', are good for wellbeing. Among the findings is that large aquatic
views which include elements of flora are particularly associated with positive
emotions, which may help to explain why so many tourists are willing to pay
a premium for a room with a sea view.[19]

What the development of both Romanticism and seaside leisure demonstrates
is how fluid our perceptions of 'place' and 'space' can be, and how they
can alter as our circumstances change. What was once seen as ugly and
frightening – such as a mountain or ocean – can become deeply attractive
and beneficial to our mental health. As the landscape archaeologist Richard
Muir puts it, 'any landscape' – or for that matter seascape – 'is composed of
not only of what lies before of eyes but what lies within our heads.'[20] This
includes memories and images drawn from the things that give meaning
and purpose to our lives.

For those with creative imagination, such as poets and painters, the
natural world – including the sea – has proved an infinitely varied source of
inspiration, particularly since the rise of Romanticism. Their work has been
appreciated over the generations by large audiences who clearly share their
enthusiasm for, and attitude towards, nature. The same can also be said for
another group of artists. The sea inspired, amongst others, Wagner, Britten,
Elgar, Debussy, Mendelssohn, Sibelius, and Ravel to compose some of the
greatest and most popular works of classical music over the past 200 years.
With that in mind, we come to our next port of call.

1   Edmund Burke, *A Philosophical Enquiry into the Origin of our Ideas of the Sublime and Beautiful* (London, 1757), p. 43.
2   Ibid. pp. 52-3.
3   Thomas Burnet, *The Theory of the Earth: Containing an Account of the Original of the Earth, and of all the General Changes which it hath already undergone, or is to undergo till the Consummation of All Things* (London, 1697), pp. 94-5.
4   Joseph Addison, *The Works of the Right Honourable Joseph Addison*, vol. 5 (London: T.Cadell and W. Davies, 1811), pp. 10-1.

5   Marilyn Butler, *Romantics, Rebels and Reactionaries: English Literature and its Background 1760-1830* (Oxford: Oxford University Press, 1981), p. 2.

6   Alain Corbin (trans. Jocelyn Phelps), *The Lure of the Sea: The Discovery of the Seaside 1750-1840* (London: Penguin, 1995), p. 167.

7   Ibid., p. 165.

8   Martin Butlin and Evelyn Joll, *The Paintings of J.M.W. Turner*, revised edn, vol. 1 (New Haven and London: Yale University Press, 1984), p. 247.

9   Robert Rosenblum, 'The Abstract Sublime', *ARTnews*, 59 (February 1961).

10   Ibid.

11   Ernest J. Lovell Jr (ed.), *Medwin's Conversations of Lord Byron* (Princeton NJ: Princeton University Press, 1966), p. 118.

12   William Knight (ed.), *Journals of Dorothy Wordsworth*, vol. 1 (London and New York: Macmillan, 1897), p. 7.

13   Malcolm Guite, *Mariner: A Voyage with Samuel Taylor Coleridge* (London: Hodder & Stoughton, 2017), p. 5.

14   Samuel Taylor Coleridge, *The Statesman's Manual; or the Bible the Best Guide to Political Skill and Foresight* (London: Gale and Fenner, 1816), p. 7.

15   Richard Dawkins, *The God Delusion* (London: Transworld, 2006), pp. 31-2.

16   Iain McGilchrist, *The Master and his Emissary: The Divided Brain and the Making of the Western World* (New Haven and London: Yale University Press, 2010).

17   Adam Nicolson, *Seamanship: A Voyage Along the Wild Coasts of the British Isles* (London and New York: HarperCollins, 2004), p. 2.

18   See Peter Borsay, 'A Room with a View: Visualising the Seaside, c.1750-1914', *Transactions of the Royal Historical Society*, 23 (2013).

19   Matthew White, Amanda Smith, Kelly Humphryes, Sabine Pahl, Deborah Snelling and Michael Depledge, 'Blue Space: The importance of water for preference, affect, and restorative ratings of natural and built scenes', *Journal of Environmental Psychology*, 30 (2010).

20   Richard Muir, *Approaches to Landscape* (London: Macmillan, 1999), p. 116.

8

To Sound So Vast a Deep

From Scottish legends to Biblical psalms, we've
always understood the sea by singing about it.
Charlotte Runcie, *Salt on your Tongue*

The Enlightenment and the emergence of the Romantic Movement coincided with the flourishing of English hymnody, the influence of which continues. In the words of musicologist Andrew Gant, 'The architecture of choral worship today is supported by two great buttresses: the music of the fifty years either side of the turn of the seventeenth century, and Victorian music.'[1]

Communal singing has a long and strong tradition in both church and seafaring. While sea shanties evolved as work-songs to provide a rhythm for repetitive tasks on board ship such as hauling sails, hymns combine the offering of worship and prayer with expressions of faith. Both types of song either deliberately or unconsciously draw upon the remarkable effect of singing together to express shared feelings and create solidarity; important not only for turning a motley crew into a team capable of sailing a ship, but also for transforming a gathering of individuals with differing views and beliefs into a community of faith.

Songs, too, can shape our thinking. As anyone who has experienced an 'earworm' will know, words associated with music seem to stick in the mind. Lines from songs can become embedded in the subconscious, only to be recalled unexpectedly when an event or emotion acts as a trigger. In *The Singing Neanderthals* Steven Mithen describes how singing has a particularly strong effect on memory, as it involves both speech and melody memory and therefore more neural circuits in the brain than either the spoken word or instrumental music alone. Consequently, hymns can play a role in shaping the thought-world of worshippers, as familiar words and phrases sung by generation after generation become part of the heritage of faith.

It is sometimes said that churchgoers learn their theology through hymns, and there is more than a grain of truth in this gently implicit indictment of preachers and teachers.

Two of the great hymn-writers of Gant's earlier period are Charles Wesley and Isaac Watts, and both drew on the sea to provide rich metaphorical imagery. In 'Jesu, lover of my soul' Wesley likens living an earthly life to navigating a storm before reaching the tranquillity of Heaven:

> Jesu, lover of my soul,
> let me to thy bosom fly,
> while the nearer waters roll,
> while the tempest still is high:
> hide, me, O my Saviour hide,
> till the storm of life is past;
> safe into the haven guide,
> O receive my soul at last.

This verse was no flight of imagination. Wesley's diary for Wednesday 15 September 1736, when he was sailing back to England from Massachusetts, includes this entry:

> This is the first time I have heard a sailor confess it was a storm. We lay under our mainsail, and let the ship drive, being by conjecture about sixty leagues from Boston, upon George's Bank; though, as we hoped, past the shoals in it. The captain never troubled himself about anything; but lay snoring even in such a night as the last, though frequently called, without ever stirring, either for squalls, or soundings, or shoals.[2]

Similarly 'the father of English hymnody', Isaac Watts, made varied use of sea imagery. This was no doubt influenced by having grown up in the port city of Southampton, located on the confluence of the rivers Test and Itchen and famous for its unusual double tide which each day causes a prolonged period of high water. In 'God is a name my soul adores', Watts uses the sea to speak the power of the Creator: 'Thy voice produced the sea and spheres, / bade the waves roar', while in 'There is a land of pure delight' Watts uses the sea to represent death which, 'like a narrow sea', has to be crossed in order to reach Heaven which lies beyond, and likens the fear of death to the trepidation of a reluctant sea-traveller:

> But timorous mortals start and shrink
> to cross the narrow sea,

and linger shivering on the brink,
and fear to launch away.

In 'God is the refuge of his saints', Watts contrasts a fearful, stormy ocean where 'every nation, every shore, / trembles and dreads the swelling tide' with a stream 'whose gentle flow / makes glad the city of our God'. Based on Psalm 46, this hymn juxtaposes the biblical chaotic waters of 'the deep' with the New Jerusalem of the Book of Revelation, where the river of the water of life flows, and where 'the sea is no more'.

Another great hymn-writer from this period is John Mason, a priest in the Church of England who was greatly influenced by non-conformity. Mason's hymn 'How shall I sing that majesty' is an eloquent attempt to express the inexpressible, ineffable nature of God. Clearly shaped by natural theology, Mason's view of God is summed-up in the verse:

How great a being, Lord, is thine,
which doth all beings keep!
Thy knowledge is the only line
to sound so vast a deep:
thou art a sea without a shore,
a sun without a sphere;
thy time is now and evermore,
thy place is everywhere.

If the seventeenth century produced some great hymns that have stood the test of time, the nineteenth century witnessed an explosion of hymn writing. This was also the age of the advent of steamships, which led to sea travel for pleasure, mass-migration across oceans, and a renewed burst of missionary activity. Millions of people experienced life at sea, whether it was a day trip on a paddle steamer, a journey to start a new life abroad, or on a mission to spread the gospel.

This new awareness and shared experience of the sea provided a rich source of inspiration for hymn-writers. This is particularly apparent in the blossoming of Protestant hymn writing in the United States, which is not surprising given the importance of sea travel in the growth of the nation. Nineteenth-century American hymnody includes 'Master, the tempest is raging!', 'My pilot is Jesus', 'The harbour bell', 'The mercy of God is an ocean divine', and 'O Maker of the mighty deep'. The writer of the latter, Presbyterian Henry J. van Dyke, Professor of English Literature at Princeton University and later American ambassador to the Netherlands and Luxembourg, picks up the ancient symbol of Christians in boats sailing in treacherous waters:

> O Maker of the mighty deep
> whereon our vessels fare,
> above our life's adventure keep
> thy faithful watch and care.
> *In thee we trust, what'er befall;*
> *thy sea is great, our boats are small.*

Similarly, the popular Sunday-school hymn 'Will your anchor hold in the storms of life?', written by Methodist schoolteacher, Priscilla J. Owens, is a product of mass movement by sea. Owens lived in the east coast port city of Baltimore, a major entry point for those arriving into the United States. In 1882, the year the hymn was written, a record 41,739 immigrants arrived in Baltimore, mostly from Europe, and some may have been among the first to sing the lines:

> Will your anchor hold in the storms of life,
> when the clouds unfold their wings of strife?
> When the strong tides lift and the cables strain,
> will your anchor drift, or firm remain?

Members of this maritime community perhaps understood first hand, or from stories doing the rounds, the struggle to keep a ship firmly anchored during a storm and the reassurance that a secure anchorage gives:

> We have an anchor that keeps the soul
> steadfast and sure while the billows roll,
> fastened to the Rock which cannot move,
> grounded firm and deep in the Saviour's love.

The influence of sea is also apparent on hymns written on this side of the Atlantic, including those for use on board ship. In a collection of *Hymns for the Sea* compiled in 1865, 'A Clergyman of the Church of England' writes of how these hymns 'express the feelings which may be supposed to be awakened in the devout heart amidst the scenes which the sea in its varying aspects presents, whether in storm or calm'.[3] There is no better or more famous example of a sailors' hymn than 'Eternal Father, strong to save', which has been adopted as the 'navy hymn' for both Britain and the United States. Written in 1860 by William Whiting, a teacher at Winchester College Choristers' School, it was initially intended as a poem for one of his pupils who was about to sail to America. Whiting drew on the images of the Holy Spirit brooding over chaotic waters at creation and of Christ stilling the storm:

> Most Holy Spirit! Who didst brood
> Upon the chaos dark and rude,
> And bid its angry tumult cease,
> And give, for wild confusion, peace;
> Oh, hear us when we cry to Thee,
> For those in peril on the sea!

The drama of Whiting's words is enhanced by John Dykes' tune '*Melita*' (an ancient name for Malta, the site of St Paul's shipwreck), making this one of the most evocative hymns in the English language. It has proved so popular that additional verses have been written over the years for divers, submariners, the US Coast Guard, naval nurses, and others.

If mass sea travel was one reason for the proliferation of sea imagery in Victorian hymns, another was the influence of the Romantic Movement. This is evident across the theological spectrum, with both Protestant and Catholic hymn-writers drawn to using language akin to Romantic poetry to express ways in which they felt connected to God through nature. One such person was Horatius Bonar, the Church of Scotland minister known as the 'prince of Scottish hymn-writers', whose hymn 'O wide embracing, wondrous love!' includes the verse:

> O wide embracing, wondrous love!
> We read thee in the sky above,
> We read thee in the earth below,
> In seas that swell, and streams that flow.

It was said of Bonar at his memorial service in 1889 that:

> His hymns were written in very varied circumstances, sometimes timed by the tinkling brook that babbled near him; sometimes attuned to the ordered tramp of the ocean, whose crested waves broke on the beach by which he wandered; sometimes set to the rude music of the railway train that hurried him to the scene of duty; sometimes measured by the silent rhythm of the midnight stars that shone above him.[4]

The influence of Romanticism is also evident in 'O worship the King all glorious above!' Based on Psalm 104, the hymn speaks of God's greatness as perceived through the natural world:

> The earth with its store of wonders untold,
> Almighty, thy power hath founded of old,
> hath' stablish'd it fast by a changeless decree,
> and round it hath cast, like a mantle, the sea.

The imagery of land being wrapped around by the sea like a mantle refers to an outer-garment that was fashionable in the eighteenth and nineteenth centuries – an idea that perhaps owes much to the thought-world of its writer, Sir Robert Grant, an evangelical Christian who served as an MP in Scotland and England and later became governor of Bombay. Born in India in 1779, Robert was the son of Charles Grant, chairman of directors of the great trading organisation the East India Company, and a prominent figure closely associated with the influential evangelical group the Clapham Sect. Robert Grant not only sailed from India to Britain as a child, making the return journey later in life, but was well aware from his association with the East India Company of the importance of the sea for transporting essential commodities and enjoyable luxuries. Such awareness may well explain the protective image of the sea in the hymn.

'O love that wilt not let me go', by the Church of Scotland minister and theologian George Matheson combines two mystical images: the soul as water, mingling with God, represented by the waters of the deep:

> O love that wilt not let me go,
> I rest my weary soul in thee;
> I give thee back the life I owe,
> that in thine ocean depths its flow
> may richer, fuller be.

This deeply moving hymn was written by Matheson on the night of his sister's marriage, an event which apparently triggered a powerful and painful memory of being jilted by the woman he loved when she discovered he was going blind. As well as displaying elements of Romanticism, Matheson, who as a student at Glasgow University studied classics, logic, and philosophy, harks back to early Christian mysticism and Neo-Platonism, with its emphasis on a mystical union with God.

The influence of Romanticism is most apparent in Anglo-Catholic hymnody. Aesthetics played an important part of the liturgical reforms inspired by the Oxford Movement, with its emphasis on Neo-Gothic architecture, ritual, and vestments, and the beauty of nature provided rich inspiration. John Keble has been described as 'the poet' of the Oxford

Movement. His hymn 'Sun of my soul, thou Saviour dear' concludes with a prayer that speaks of union with the divine and God's love as an ocean. Like Matheson, Keble also drew on both Romanticism and Neo-Platonism to evoke a sense of God's love as unbounded and immeasurable, in which we can become surrounded and lost, like a sailor or swimmer in a vast sea:

> Come near and bless us when we wake,
> Ere through the world our way we take;
> Till in the ocean of thy love
> We lose ourselves in heaven above.

A student at Oxford whose poetry was praised by Keble was F. W. Faber, an Anglo-Catholic who later converted to Roman Catholicism and went on to become a significant hymn-writer. Faber was clearly influenced by the Romantic Movement, counting William Wordsworth among his friends. Faber uses the sea as a metaphor for our inability to appreciate the immensity of God's love in his hymn 'There's a wideness in God's mercy / like the wideness of the sea' which later continues, 'For the love of God is broader / than the measure of man's mind.'

Faber, like many contemporaries influenced by Romanticism, drew on a sense of the sublime evoked by the sea. For other hymn-writers, it was the peril of life at sea that provided a metaphor for confronting difficulties in life and faith. This has a particular resonance for those who lived in times when awareness of the trials and tribulations of sea-travel was much greater than our own. Cecil Frances Alexander is one of the best-known hymn-writers of the nineteenth century. The wife of an Anglican bishop in Ireland, she was greatly influenced both by the rise of Anglo-Catholicism (Keble edited an anthology of her hymns) and the natural world, most evidently in 'All things bright and beautiful'. In 'Jesus calls us: o'er the tumult', Alexander draws on the sea's violence, terror and power to destroy – things that put us at the mercy of forces beyond our control – alluding to Christ calling his disciples on the Sea of Galilee:

> Jesus calls us: o'er the tumult
> of our life's wild restless sea,
> day by day his sweet voice soundeth,
> saying, 'Christian follow me'.

The sea also plays a prominent role in Roman Catholic hymnody, drawing on the medieval image of Mary as *Stella Maris*, Star of the Sea. The reason for the association of Mary with the sea is unclear, though it may be as simple as the similarity of their names in Latin: *Maria* (Mary) and *mare* (sea). F.W. Faber's devotion to Mary is evident in his hymn 'O purest of creatures', which also uses the turbulent sea as a metaphor for the difficulties faced by the Church:

> Deep night hath come down on this rough-spoken world,
> And the banners of darkness are boldly unfurled;
> And the tempest-tossed Church, – all her eyes are on thee;
> *They look to thy shining, sweet Star of the Sea!*

An important figure in popularising such hymns is Richard Runciman Terry, the first Director of Music at Westminster Cathedral. Terry played a leading role in developing choral music in the Roman Catholic Church in the first decades of the twentieth century, and was the editor of the influential and widely-used *Westminster Hymnal*, first published in 1912. Of the thirty hymns Terry included in the section of the hymnal for the Blessed Virgin Mary, seven refer to the sea. Typical of this genre is 'Ave, Maria! O Maiden, O Mother', which includes the verse:

> *Ave Maria!* Thou portal of heaven
> harbour of refuge, to thee do we flee
> lost in the darkness, by stormy winds driven
> shine on our darkness, fair star of the sea.
> *Mater amabilis, ore pro nobis*
> pray for thy children who call upon thee
> *Ave sanctissima! Ave purissima!*
> Sinless and beautiful, Star of the sea.

The image here is of Heaven as a sanctuary from the trials of life, just as a harbour is a haven for sailors in a storm. Mary is the intercessor who offers the most efficacious prayers to God that we may reach that destination. Like so many others, Terry's awareness of the sea came from personal engagement rather than abstract thought. Born and brought up near the Northumberland coast, Terry was part of a long-established seafaring family. He even edited a collection of sea shanties, and in the introduction to *The Shanty Book* Terry describes his life-long love of these songs, his seafaring background, and his enjoyment of sailing, which clearly shaped his religious faith as well.

All the hymns mentioned so far make explicit reference to the sea. Intriguingly, some of the most enduringly popular hymns make no such reference and yet were composed as a direct consequence of a profound personal experience of the sea. This includes what is perhaps the best-known and best-loved nature hymn, 'How great thou art'. As well as being steeped in natural theology, the hymn makes a connection between the work of God as Creator and Jesus as Saviour, moving from its first verse:

> O Lord, my God, when I in awesome wonder
> Consider all the worlds Thy Hands have made
> I see the stars, I hear the rolling thunder
> Thy power throughout the universe displayed

to the second:

> And when I think of God, His Son not sparing
> Sent Him to die, I scarce can take it in
> That on the Cross, my burden gladly bearing
> He bled and died to take away my sin

The underlying message is that if God deserves our praise for what we experience in the natural world then so, too, should we give thanks for the saving work of Jesus Christ, as expressed in the chorus:

> *Then sings my soul, my Saviour God, to Thee*
> *How great Thou art, how great Thou art*
> *Then sings my soul, my Saviour God, to Thee*
> *How great Thou art, how great Thou art*

'How great thou art' is based on a poem, 'O Sture Gud' ('O Great God'), written in 1885 by the Swedish writer, poet, politician, and sailor, Carl Boberg. Boberg wrote the poem after experiencing a sudden and dramatic storm on his way back from a church service. The storm and the peaceful calm which followed, which Boberg observed looking out from his home over Mönsterås Bay, proved inspirational. As Boberg later wrote:

> It was that time of year when everything seemed to be in its richest colouring; the birds were singing in trees and everywhere. It was very warm; a thunderstorm appeared on the horizon and soon thunder and lightning. We had to hurry to shelter. But the storm was soon over and the clear sky appeared.
>
> When I came home I opened my window toward the sea. There evidently had been a funeral and the bells were playing the tune of 'When eternity's clock calling my saved soul to its Sabbath rest.' That evening, I wrote the song, 'O Store Gud.'[5]

Perhaps the best-known account of an explicitly religious experience at sea that inspired a hymn which makes no mention of what lay behind it is that of

John Newton's conversion on board a stricken ship during and after a storm in 1748. Newton experienced life at sea as a teenager, having been press-ganged into the navy. His eventual attraction to life at sea, when he left the navy to join the slave trade, was such that he was willing to be separated from his wife and childhood sweetheart Polly, for whom he once deserted ship and risked execution. By all accounts, Newton relished the life of a sailor, and lived a lifestyle far removed from that which his pious mother had hoped for. In doing so he rejected the religion of his youth. However, Newton's life took a dramatic turn at the age of 39 during a storm in the north Atlantic when sailing for Liverpool on board the *Greyhound*. Newton had been deeply and volubly anti-religious, which perhaps shows an underlying fascination with religion akin to Conrad's description of a love-hate relationship with the sea. Describing events during the storm, Newton wrote:

> About nine o'clock, being almost spent with cold and labor, I went to speak with the captain, who was busied elsewhere; and just as I was returning from him I said, almost without meaning, 'If this will not do, the Lord have mercy on us.' This (though spoken with little reflection) was the first desire I had breathed for mercy for the space of many years.[6]

The irreligious Newton had prayed. Over the next few days, as the ship limped to safety but in danger of running out of food and water, Newton prayed more, and rediscovered his childhood faith. As he later wrote, '*I began to know that there is a God who hears and answers prayer.*'[7] Newton likened his conversion to St Paul's, as that of someone who was bent on destroying the faith which he later embraced. Newton's religious experience at sea underlies the words of his famous hymn 'Amazing grace', as he believed it was by God's grace that he was not only spared his life at sea, but that he had been given salvation from his dissolute and faithless existence:

> Through many dangers, toils and snares
> I have already come:
> 'tis grace has brought me safe thus far
> And grace will lead me home

Famously, it took several years from his conversion for Newton to renounce the evil slave trade in which he was engaged, after which he became one of its most passionate and effective opponents.

Another great figure who found inspiration at sea, yet did not mention this in the hymn it spawned, was F.W. Faber's hero, John Henry Newman, one of the leaders of the Oxford Movement who later became a cardinal in the Roman Catholic Church. On 8 December 1832, Newman, then a young Anglican priest, left England for the first time. He was sailing from Falmouth on board the *Hermes* destined for the Mediterranean, accompanying his close friend Hurrell Froude and his father, Archdeacon R. H. Froude. Hurrell Froude was suffering from advanced tuberculosis, and this trip to the Mediterranean was for health reasons. The severity of Froude's illness may explain why they went at this time of year: avoiding a harsh English winter meant experiencing the worst time of year for sailing.

The trip took them to Gibraltar, Malta, Greece, Sicily, Naples, and Rome. In April, Newman decided to travel back to Sicily via Naples, while the Froudes continued to Marseille. Newman wanted solitude and 'to commune with high nature', a comment that shows how deeply he had been influenced by Romanticism, He did not travel alone, however. He had met a Neapolitan, Gennaro, who had served on the *Victory* in the Battle of Trafalgar, and who accompanied Newman as his servant.

In Sicily, Newman contracted typhoid and became seriously ill and delirious. As he recovered, Newman decided to return to England. The story continues in Newman's words:

> Before starting from my inn in the morning of May 26th or 27th, I sat down on my bed and began to sob bitterly. My servant, who had acted as my nurse, asked what ailed me. I could only answer, 'I have a work to do in England.'
>
> I was aching to get home; yet for want of a vessel I was kept at Palermo for three weeks. I began to visit the Churches, and they calmed my impatience, though I did not attend any services. I knew not the presence of the Blessed Sacrament there. At last I got off in an orange boat, bound for Marseilles. We were becalmed a whole week in the Straits of Bonifacio. There it was that I wrote the lines, 'Lead, kindly light,' which have since become well known.[8]

At the time, Newman called the hymn 'The pillar of cloud', an allusion to the story in Exodus of the Israelites travelling through the wilderness guided by a pillar of cloud by day and a pillar of fire by night. The hymn is about the journey of faith, of making that journey step-by-step: 'I do not ask to see / the distant scene – one step enough for me.' The hymn also speaks of the trials that are faced on that journey, represented by the wild terrain that must be crossed: 'o'er moor and fen, o'er crag and torrent, till the night is gone'.

Newman does not mention the sea but its presence is palpable, providing the wilderness in which Newman currently found himself.

In the hymn, Newman relates his longing to return to England to a longing to be with God, and of surrendering one's will to God. The context was ripe for such reflection: having been seriously ill, Newman had recently confronted the possibility of death, and his sense of mortality was reinforced by travelling with a close friend whose life was near its end. Away from England for the first time, stuck at sea, Newman felt dislocated and insecure. Reflecting much later about writing the hymn, Newman gave a glimpse of his emotional condition at the time, speaking of 'the transient states of mind which come upon one when homesick or seasick, or in any other way sensitive or excited.' Interestingly, 'Lead kindly light' was set to music by John Dykes, the composer of '*Melita*', and is still often sung to his tune '*Lux Benigna*'.

The connection between the sea and confronting death, again without mentioning the sea, lies behind one of the most popular hymns for funerals, memorial services, and many solemn – and even sporting – events: 'Abide with me'. In the summer of 1847, its writer, Henry Francis Lyte, was seriously ill with tuberculosis. Lyte had served as the perpetual curate of the fishing port of Lower Brixham in South Devon for twenty-three years, and was well-known for both his writing and his pastoral care of the local seafaring community. Terminally ill (Lyte died in France later that year), he would frequently go to his favourite spot in the garden of his home, Berry Head House, overlooking Torbay, where, according to his biographer, 'he would sit and contemplate the ever-changing face of the deep'.[9] It was here, as the sun was setting, that Lyte found the inspiration for his last and greatest hymn:

> Abide with me; fast falls the eventide;
> the darkness deepens; Lord, with me abide!
> when other helpers fail, and comforts flee,
> help of the helpless, O abide with me.

The hymn draws deeply from Lyte's awareness of his own mortality, but also his sense of immortality. Some years earlier he had a life-changing experience, when he had a vision of his friend, the Reverend John Pattison, who appeared to Lyte at his death telling Lyte he had 'passed into another state'. From then on Lyte had a profound sense of death as the gateway to another existence. And so as well as the connotations of death with the setting sun, the unmentioned sea provides the backdrop of the sense of the eternal as

Lyte sought God's presence in the evening of his life. Lyte's personal situation makes this hymn all the more poignant as well as profound.

⌒

Few hymn-writers today make such use of the sea. This is understandable, given the relative decline of sea travel since its heyday in the nineteenth century. Many people today will have experienced strong turbulence in an airplane, few will have been caught up in a storm crossing the Atlantic. Nevertheless, hymns endure and so today's worshippers continue to be fed by thoughts and ideas dating back a hundred years or more, and to images beyond the direct experience of most people.

The longevity of hymns not only brings with it an insight into the concerns of previous generations, but ensures that worshippers continue to be influenced by natural theology, Neo-Platonism, and the appreciation of the sublime associated with Romanticism. Explicitly or implicitly, these hymns have shaped the thinking of generations of worshippers, who have been infused with images and metaphors of the sea, as well as direct references to both its awe-inspiring and terrifying nature.

The similarity of many of these hymns – the product of different churches, denominations, and theological traditions – is also significant. Whether Catholic or Protestant, High or Low Church, theologically liberal or conservative, the spiritual impact of the sea appears to be universal. The commonality of religious experience associated with the sea, and with the natural world more generally, is what lies behind the shift that took place in natural theology in the second half of the nineteenth century. If Darwinism led to the demise of one approach to natural theology, as we shall now see, a growing appreciation of nature led to the emergence of another.

1   Andrew Gant, *O Sing Unto the Lord: A History of English Church Music* (London: Profile Press, 2015), p. 331.
2   Charles Wesley (ed. J. Telford) *The Journal of the Rev. Charles Wesley. The Early Journal, 1736-1739* (London: Robert Culley, 1910), p. 76.
3   A Clergyman of the Church of England (ed.), *Hymns for the Sea* (London: J and C Mozley, 1865), p. v.
4   Norman Mable, *Popular Hymns and Their Writers*, 2nd edn (London: Independent Press, 1951) p. 45.
5   Quoted in Michael Ireland, 'Veleky Bog: How Great is Our God! The story behind how a thunderstorm in Sweden prompted the writing of How Great Thou Art, one of Christianity's greatest and much-loved hymns, ASSIST News Service (Sunday, October 7, 2007); http://www.assistnews.net/Stories/2007/s07100068.htm.
6   *The Life of the Rev John Newton, Rector of St Mary Woolnoth, London* (New York: American Tract Society, 1830), p. 42.

7   John Newton, *'Out of the Depths': An Autobiography* (Chicago: Moody Press, no date), p. 79.

8   John Henry Newman, *Apologia Pro Vita Sua: Being A Reply to a Pamphlet entitled 'What, then, does Dr Newman mean?'* (New York: D.Appleton and Co., 1865), p. 83.

9   Henry James Garland, *Henry Francis Lyte and the Story of 'Abide with Me'* (Manchester: Torch pulishing, n.d.), p. 77.

9

The Oceanic Feeling

The voice of the sea speaks to the soul
Kate Chopin, *The
Awakening*

Gerard Manley Hopkins is widely regarded as one of the great poets of the nineteenth century. His style of writing was idiosyncratic, which probably explains why most of Hopkins' best poetry was published posthumously, and that he was recognised as a major poet only after his death. However, his first published poem, 'Winter with the Gulf Stream', was written when Hopkins was aged 18, and includes this description of the sun setting over the western sea:

> The webbed and the watery west
> Where yonder crimson fireball sets
> Looks laid for feasting and for rest.
>
> I see long reefs of violets
> In beryl-covered ferns so dim,
> A gold-water Pactolus frets
>
> Its brindled wharves and yellow brim,
> The waxen colours weep and run,
> And slendering to his burning rim
>
> Into the flat blue mist the sun
> Drops out and the day is done.

Much of Hopkins' poetry was inspired by nature, and in particular his awareness of God through the natural world. 'The world is charged with the grandeur of God', he wrote, and constantly speaks of the divine to those with

the ability to perceive it. Each natural object, he argued, possesses an identity
or essence that he called 'inscape' which can have an effect on the beholder
which he termed 'instress'. Together, inscape and instress lead to God:

> The birds sing to him, the thunder speaks of his terror, the lion is like
> his strength, the sea is like his greatness, the honey is like his sweetness;
> they are something like him, they make him known, they tell of him,
> they give him glory, but they do not know that they do, they do not
> know him, they never can … But man can know God, can mean to
> give him glory.[1]

Although not appreciated at the time, Hopkins was contributing to a new
approach to natural theology. Hopkins was not viewing the natural world
and seeking God with the eyes of a scientist, but was nevertheless profoundly
affected by nature both psychologically and spiritually. As Iain McGilchrist
says of Hopkins, 'almost everything … suggests a right hemisphere
dominance' in his disposition towards the world.[2]

This disposition led to Hopkins writing some of the most profound
religious poetry in the English language; and yet the faith that underpinned
so much of his work almost stopped his career as a poet from developing.
As a young man and when a student at Oxford, Hopkins had been a prolific
poet. However, his religious convictions at first led him to turn away from
poetry. Brought up a High Church Anglican, Hopkins was received into the
Roman Catholic Church in his early twenties by John Henry Newman, and
two years later began to train for ordination as a Jesuit priest. At this point
Hopkins regarded poetry as a distraction from his religious calling, and so
he burned all his poems and vowed never to write again unless requested to
do so by a higher authority.

Hopkins' return to poetry came seven years later, in 1875, when the
superior of his religious community asked him to write a poem about the
sinking of the ship the *Deutschland*. Sailing from Bremen to New York, the
Deutschland foundered at the mouth of the Thames on 7 December 1872.
Although it took twenty-four hours to sink no early rescue was attempted,
and many perished. Among them were five Franciscan nuns fleeing the anti-
clerical Falk Laws in Germany, who provided for Hopkins a focus as he
pondered one of the most enduring and puzzling questions of theodicy:
how can a God of love allow suffering? In 'The Wreck of the Deutschland',
the awesome power of the sea speaks of God as the giver and taker of life:

I admire thee, master of the tides,
Of the Yore-flood, of the year's fall;
The recurb and the recovery of the gulf's sides,
The girth of it and the wharf of it and the wall;
Stanching, quenching ocean of a motionable mind;
Ground of being, and granite of it: past all
Grasp God, throned behind
Death with a sovereignty that heeds but hides, bodes but abides.

In Hopkins' mind, suffering and death could only make sense in relation to Christ's suffering and death. For Hopkins, the only plausible explanation for the five nuns' fate is their union with Christ:

Five! the finding and sake
And cipher of suffering Christ.
Mark, the mark is of man's make
And the word of it Sacrificed.
But he scores it in scarlet himself on his own bespoken,
Before-time-taken, dearest prizèd and priced –
Stigma, signal, cinquefoil token
For lettering of the lamb's fleece, ruddying of the rose-flake.

For Hopkins, the sea's dangerous, capricious nature was strangely alluring, breaking his long silence and inspiring perhaps his greatest work. The poem may also owe something to a preoccupation with danger at sea as his father, Manley Hopkins, who was also an accomplished poet, ran a family marine-insurance business. Whatever the impetus, 'The Wreck of the Deutschland' released Gerard Manley Hopkins' suppressed creativity.

The effect of the sea on the mind is something that fascinated the psychiatrist and founder of analytical psychology, Carl Jung. As a child, Jung had an experience that later influenced his work on personality. Brought up in landlocked Switzerland, Jung describes not the call of the sea but that of a close freshwater relative, the third largest lake in Europe:

My mother took me to Thurgan to visit friends, who had a castle on Lake Constance. I could not be dragged away from the water. The waves from the steamer washed up to the shore, the sun glistened on the water, and the sand under the water had been curled into little ridges by the waves. The lake stretched away into the distance. This expanse of water was an inconceivable pleasure to me, an incomparable splendour. At that time the idea became fixed in my mind that I must live near a lake; without water, I thought, nobody could live at all.[3]

Later in life Jung came to realise that vast expanses of water can have a profound psychological effect, so much so that he regarded it as one of the most powerful images in dreams. 'The sea', he wrote, 'is the container of the unknown and the mysterious. It is an appropriate synonym for the unconscious.'[4] He also wrote, 'The sea is the symbol of the collective unconscious because it hides unsuspected depths under a reflecting surface.'[5] For Jung, the collective unconscious meant that it is not something personal to an individual but common throughout humanity. Jung believed that the sea speaks to everyone who encounters it about what lies hidden deep within us. For Jung, the call of the sea is therefore fundamentally a call to explore our own hidden depths.

While it is undoubtedly the case that the sea can have a powerful effect on the mind, could it also be that its attraction has a physiological explanation? There are several intriguing suggestions that currently defy scientific verification. One is that, as the human body comprises about four-fifths water, we have a special affinity with the sea because, like the sea, we are subject the same changes of the gravitational force of the moon that creates tides. There are many myths that link changes in human behaviour with the ebb and flow of the tide that long predate an understanding of human physiology and the force of gravity.

Another common suggestion is that the sea is associated with a hidden memory of our experience before birth. Can the attraction of the sea have something to do with a deep desire for security in our subconscious? Does the visceral experience of plunging into water and swimming take us back deep in our subconscious to our mother's womb? The sensation of swimming or floating in water is certainly the nearest we can get to recreating the conditions of floating in amniotic fluid in the womb. In his book *Waterlog*, the fanatical swimmer Roger Deakin described swimming in such terms. 'These amniotic waters are both utterly safe and yet terrifying, for at birth anything could go wrong', he wrote. 'This may account for the anxieties every swimmer experiences in deep water… The swimmer experiences the terror and the bliss of being born.'[6]

Another explanation of our attraction to the sea stems not from our experience before birth, but from our very distant origins as sea creatures. It is often noted that the primacy of the creation of sea creatures in the Genesis account of the creation of the Earth resonates with our scientific understanding of life originating in the sea. This has led to the suggestion that Genesis and other ancient creation stories tap into a subconscious awareness of our aquatic origins. This theory appealed to the novelist and keen sailor John Steinbeck, who called the effect 'sea-memory'. Observing that the human foetus has the physical reminders of our aquatic ancestry in the form of vestigial gills, he speculated whether there might also be psychological reminders deep within our subconscious, that stimulate a desire to return to our aquatic origins. Mary Oliver expresses this sense of deep connection beautifully succinctly in her poem 'At the Edge of the Ocean':

> I have heard this music before,
> saith the body.

Another trigger for sea-memory has been suggested in relation to the 'aquatic ape' or 'aquatic adaptation' theory. This was postulated by the marine biologist Alister Hardy when Professor of Zoology at the University of Oxford, and first appeared in a paper published in *New Scientist* in 1960. Subsequently it was developed and popularised in books by Elaine Morgan. Hardy argued that a principal difference between humans and other apes stems from our ancestors returning to live by the sea in search of food. In competing for food, Hardy argued, our distant ancestors were driven to search on seashores and in coastal waters. In doing so, *homo sapiens* evolved into streamlined, hairless creatures kept warm by sub-cutaneous fat who became, unlike any other ape, good at swimming and diving, and who walked on two legs so as to be able to wade into shallow water to search for food. 'The graceful shape of Man – or woman! – is most striking when compared with the clumsy form of the ape', wrote Hardy, perhaps somewhat tongue in cheek. 'All the curves of the human body have the beauty of a well-designed boat.'[7] Hardy, who was an accomplished diver, further speculated, 'Does this idea perhaps explain the satisfaction that so many people feel in going to the seaside, in bathing, and indulging in various forms of aquatic sport? Does not the vogue of the aqua-lung indicate a latent urge in Man to swim beneath the surface?'[8]

Hardy's hypothesis has remained controversial, as it challenges the widely held view that humans evolved bipedalism on the savannahs of Africa. Nevertheless, it has gained traction, as evidenced from David Attenborough's two programmes on *The Waterside Ape* broadcast on BBC Radio in 2016.

If Hardy, Morgan, and Steinbeck are correct, the call of the sea because of its 'otherness' is really an illusion. What pulls us away from the familiar and relatively safe existence on land is not so much a desire for something different to normality, but a residual attraction to what was once our natural habitat. This offers freedom, but not the freedom of escapism. Instead it leads to the freedom created from a sense of belonging, of being 'at home', where we are free to be who we truly are. But, of course, we are no longer aquatic and have returned to the land; and just as the residual collective memory of the threat of predators may be linked to fear, anxiety, and our 'fight or flight' response to danger, the same may also be true for the threat of flooding, tsunamis, or drowning.

If the aquatic ape theory is correct, our epigenetic connection to the sea is just as Catullus and Joseph Conrad describe – *odi et amo* – as we feel simultaneously connected with, and disconnected from, the marine environment. This ambiguity is expressed in the widespread stories of half-human, half-fish mermaids, and selkies, who can change from being seals to being human by shedding their skin. These stories often have a strong element of sexual attraction and desire, yet often with sad or fatal outcomes for those who try to move from sea to land or vice versa.

⌒

When Hardy retired as a marine biologist he turned his attention to his other lifelong interest, religion. Hardy had no difficulty in reconciling religious beliefs with scientific enquiry, and regarded both as rational human activities that could be mutually enriching. Hardy was fascinated by the nature and purpose of religious experience and wanted to gain a better understanding of it. His interest at least in part stemmed from personal experience. Writing shortly before his death, Hardy described the following childhood experience:

> Just occasionally when I was sure no-one was could see me, I became so overcome with the glory of the natural scene that for a moment or two I fell on my knees in prayer – not prayer asking for anything, but thanking God, who felt very real to me, for the glories of his kingdom and for allowing me to feel them. It was always by the running waterside that I did this, perhaps in front of a great foam of Meadow Sweet or a mass of Purple Loosestrife.[9]

In 1969, Hardy established the Religious Experience Research Unit at Manchester College, Oxford (now Harris Manchester College), to conduct a major scientific study of people's religious experiences. Now renamed the Religious Experience Research Centre and relocated to the University of Wales, Trinity St David at Lampeter, it houses a database of anonymous, personal accounts of religious experiences which Hardy and others have collected and analysed.

Of the 6,000 or so accounts in the database, 81 are experiences closely associated with the sea. They fall into two main categories, which are consistent with the categories of other religious experiences associated with nature found in the database. One group refers to events on board a ship or boat in times of danger, including accounts by sailors from the Second World War. The respondents describe sensing the close presence of God and a feeling of peace and security that overcomes fear. As one respondent commented, 'I feel increasingly ... a sense of being guided and protected by a power beyond myself. This has applied in major events, as in the sea off Dunkirk in 1940, when I felt detached from events and assured that I was safe.'[10]

Others, too, have described the spiritual dimension of facing danger at sea. In 1947, the Norwegian explorer and anthropologist Thor Heyerdahl crossed the Pacific from Peru to Polynesia in a balsa-raft, the *Kon-Tiki*, to demonstrate the possibility of his theory that long ago people from South America had settled on the Polynesian islands, arriving on similar craft. While the voyage was successful, it was not without incident. Writing later about hitting a reef where 'the surf pulled and tore at me, and the whole ocean tried to drag me away from where I was clinging' Heyerdahl commented that he 'had taken a brief glimpse behind the veil of life and experienced a sensation that something was going on there.' Heyerdahl's interpretation of his experience was not of an external divine assistance, but the discovery of unknown powers deep within:

> I had promised myself that if we all survived the towering wall of waves I would never forget that moment ...Where had the extra power that I had begged for in the face of death come from? The white birds that flew across the blue sky as we lay and regained our breath on the beach reminded me of the doves of Christianity bringing messages from Heaven. But the help that I felt as a physical force out there in the ocean had not come from above; it came from within. Perhaps Heaven with a capital H of the Bible and Koran should not be mistaken for heaven with a small h that we can all find within us?[11]

The other common experience described in the Religious Experience database is very different, but no less powerful. The accounts are remarkably similar and describe how, when walking alone along a deserted beach or coastline and looking out to sea, the respondent had an overwhelming sense of the existence of a Creator and of being united with the rest of creation. This is something John Steinbeck reflected on during a 4,000-mile voyage round the Gulf of California, or Sea of Cortez, in 1940, with his friend and marine biologist Ed Ricketts. In *The Log from the Sea of Cortez*, Steinbeck comments:

> it is a strange thing that most of the feeling we call religious, most of the mystical outcrying which is one of the most prized and used and desired reactions in our species, is really the understanding and the attempt to say that man is related to the whole thing, related inextricably to all reality, known and unknowable.[12]

Such 'mystical' experiences verge on pantheism – of sensing God not only as Creator but *within* creation. This is also apparent in the accounts of experiences collected by Hardy, including the following experience that took place on the west coast of Wales:

> I was walking, alone, towards the sunset along the very fine cliffs and finally stopped and sat looking out to sea, to watch the last moments of the sun's descent. I remember that the sky was immensely, profoundly blue and continued perfectly clear as the sun's light waned, and I distinctly recall this gave me a powerful sense of infinity, a reminder of huge tracts of space and galaxies many light years away... I also remember noticing the golden path of the sun on a calmish sea and the many signs around of the interaction of rock and water, the worn hollows and spines of one and the ceaseless movement of the other. It was from this observation that my mind began to move in the direction of religious thought, but that is perhaps a misleading way of expressing the fact. The strongest memory I have is of a conviction pressing in on my whole being, not merely my mind, that the creation in front of me, its elemental forces, its huge complexity was not complete or self-sufficient, but that behind it, within it, was the Creator or ultimate Reality.[13]

Towards the end of the nineteenth century, the Harvard philosopher and psychologist William James undertook the first significant study of religious experience. His findings were delivered in the Gifford Lectures of 1901-2 at Edinburgh University and published simultaneously as *The Varieties of Religious Experience*. His lectures are regarded as perhaps the most influential and thought-provoking in the history of this prestigious series on natural theology, and his book, while controversial and not without its critics, remains a pre-eminent work in its field. James' research involved collecting and analysing accounts of mystical experiences from which he identified four defining characteristics. For James, a religious experience is *ineffable*, defying description in words; it has a *noetic quality*, giving insight into a deeper truth; it is *transient*, lasting only minutes or seconds; and is *passive*, creating the sense of being out of control and under the influence of a superior power.

Among the examples James cites are several centred on the sea. Perhaps his choice was influenced by his own travels across the Atlantic, but what is for sure is that he identified the two common experiences associated with the sea that are found in the Religious Experience database. The first – a sense of well-being in the face of extreme danger – is well expressed in an account by a sailor, Frank Bullen, who converted to Christianity on board ship and who wrote his autobiography with the title *With Christ at Sea*. When suspended over the sea, upside down, by one foot from a broken boom, Bullen describes feeling 'high exultation in my certainty of eternal life ... I suppose I could have hung there no more than five seconds, but in that time I lived a whole age of delight.'[14]

A very different account cited by James is by the German writer Malwida von Meysenbug, who, after years of being unable to pray, found herself on a seashore when 'I was impelled to kneel down ... before the illimitable ocean, symbol of the Infinite. I felt that I prayed as I had never prayed before and knew what prayer really is: to return from the solitude of individuation into the consciousness of unity with all that is.'[15]

Among von Meysenbug's acquaintances was the French Nobel Prize winning writer and dramatist Romain Rolland, who, like James, was fascinated by psychology and religion. Rolland devoted himself to studying Eastern mysticism, as well as writing at his home on the shore of Lake Geneva. From his study of Hinduism and other religions far removed from western influences (though resonant with the mysticism of Neo-Platonism), he concluded that there is such a thing as the 'oceanic feeling', which echoes with many of the accounts in the Religious Experience database, as well as that by von Meysenbug. While James focused on religious experience through brief moments of mysticism, Rolland's attention was more towards what predisposes people to be religious. He believed that the basic and almost universal religious impulse comes from feeling a sense of the infinite, which may or may not lead to the sort of profound but brief mystical experience described by von Meysenbug. The oceanic feeling could be induced by staring into the night sky, a view across a vast landscape, or by looking out to sea. The horizon, at which a vast expanse of sea meets a vast expanse of sky, is a particularly powerful symbol of the infinite and eternal, and a pointer to what lies beyond our experience or comprehension.

Although he was not a religious believer, Rolland had personal experience of the oceanic feeling and understood how it might lead to religious belief. It was the subject of a correspondence Rolland had with his friend Sigmund Freud who, in 1927, published his response in the opening section of his book *Civilization and Its Discontents*. Freud, too, acknowledged the validity of the oceanic feeling, although he said he had not experienced it himself. He disagreed, though, with Rolland over its role as a religious impulse. Freud not only dismissed Rolland's thesis, but effectively dismissed the whole notion of natural theology, in which a primary religious impulse stems from an encounter with God as Creator. In Freud's view, religiosity and a search for God stemmed not from an encounter with nature, but an instinctive 'feeling of infantile helplessness' and 'a longing for a [protective] father'.[16]

If the sea speaks of the infinite, then so too does it speak of mystery. This is also apparent from the accounts in the religious experience database. For centuries the sea was deeply mysterious, largely because its depths had hardly been explored. As Helen Rozwadowski observes in her history of deep sea exploration:

> Until the first decades of the [nineteenth] century, the location of the ocean's bottom – if it existed at all – was anyone's guess. The 1823 *Encyclopaedia Britannica* entry for 'sea' stated simply, 'Through want of instruments, the sea beyond a certain depth has been found unfathomable'.[17]

It was not until the mid-to-late nineteenth century that deep-sea surveys such as that conducted on board the *Challenger* began to unlock the mysteries of the deep.

As well as mapping the terrain of the sea-bed, so, too, has deep sea exploration and the development of oceanography increased our knowledge of sea-life. Throughout history, the sea has been regarded as the home of monsters, such as the biblical creatures Leviathan and Rahab. The submarine photography of Jacques Cousteau, and more recently the BBC's *Blue Planet*, have helped remove much of the mystery of sea life and, if anything, enhanced a sense of awe and wonder of the range of strange creatures that live in the sea. Scientific discoveries have changed our perception of the sea in other ways. Research by Henry Cavendish, James Watt, and Antoine Lavoisier in the late eighteenth century showed that water was not an element, as previously thought, but a compound of hydrogen and oxygen (though even today the chemical structure of water is not fully understood and remains an intriguing area of research). Explanations were also found for mysterious phenomena which for centuries were the source of myth and superstitions, such as phosphorescence (when marine organisms emit a glow at night), waterspouts (columns of water in a vortex above the sea), and perhaps most notably the electrical activity known as St Elmo's fire.

Despite increased knowledge and rational explanations for supposedly supernatural phenomena, the sea remains a powerful image of the mysterious and the unknown – and therefore, potentially, of God. This resonates with the argument presented by the German theologian and philosopher Rudolf Otto in his influential book *The Idea of the Holy*. After travelling extensively in North Africa and the Middle East in the early twentieth century and experiencing various forms of religion, Otto turned his attention to what he perceived to be common across religions. From his research he concluded that something universal was what he termed an experience of the 'numinous': an awareness of the presence of the divine which was often associated with fear. Otto regarded a numinous experience not merely as a psychological state, such as a sense of awe and wonder, but as an authentic religious experience which could manifest itself in very different ways: 'The feeling of it may at times come sweeping like a gentle tide', or 'may burst into sudden eruption from the depths of the soul with spasms or convulsions', or 'may be become the hushed, trembling, and speechless humility in the presence of … that which is mystery.'[18] To describe our response to the mystery that is God, Otto used the term *mysterium tremendum*, and to explain its difference from experiencing a sense of awe and wonder he cited a sermon by St John Chrysostom:

> We wonder at the greatness of the sea and its measureless expanse, but terror and 'fear' only seize upon us when we gaze down into its depths. So, too, here the Psalmist. When he gazes down into the immeasurable, yawning Depth of the divine Wisdom, dizziness comes upon him and he recoils in terrified wonder.[19]

The third key feature of the accounts in the religious experience database is the importance of solitude. All the respondents refer to being alone when their religious experience takes place. For those walking by the sea, the solitude may last only minutes or hours. Sailing can prolong and heighten the experience, and attracts those who are content without human company. As the author of *Charlotte's Web* and amateur sailor E. B. White reflected, 'I liked to sail alone. The sea was the same as a girl to me – I did not want anyone else along.'[20] For long-distance, single-handed sailors, their solitude can last weeks or months, and is similar to the experience of a hermit or solitary monk or nun, or of someone on a rigorous religious retreat. This begs the question whether sailors pushed to the limits of human endurance can offer any insights into the spiritual dimension of being alone on what Joseph Conrad called 'the majestic monotony of the sea'.[21]

The first person to sail single-handed around the world was the Canadian-born American Joshua Slocum. Slocum set sail from Boston, Massachusetts, in his boat the *Spray* on 24 April 1895, returning to Newport, Rhode Island, over three years later on 27 June 1898. Although Slocum's circumnavigation included stop-offs, the 46,000 mile voyage nevertheless involved extended periods of solitude. Soon after his return, Slocum wrote an account of his experiences and *Sailing Alone Around the World* quickly became an international best-seller. Slocum's fame spread, and he has since inspired generations of long-distance sailors.

A feature of Slocum's account is its psychological and spiritual nature. As a recent biographer observed, 'Slocum's long voyage was as much an inner voyage through the psyche as an outward voyage over ocean waters … As he stripped away the sea's layers and penetrated its mysteries, a deep spirituality awakened.'[22] The key to this awakening was what Slocum referred to as his 'solitude supreme', which only manifested itself after he confronted initial feelings of deep isolation. 'I was destined to sail once more into the depths of solitude,' he wrote, 'but these experiences had no bad effect on me; on the contrary, a spirit of charity and even benevolence grew stronger in my nature through the meditations of these supreme hours on the sea.'[23] If solitude induced in Slocum a spiritual state, it was also overtly religious. Describing sailing alone in the Pacific he wrote, 'Then was the time to uncover my head, for I sailed alone with God. The vast ocean was again around me, and the horizon was unbroken by land.'[24] Commenting on his voyage to a journalist a few years later, Slocum said, 'No man ever lived to see more of the solemnity of the depths than I have seen, and I resent, quickly, the hint that a real sea story might be other than religious.'[25]

It is interesting to compare Slocum's experiences with those of other long distance sailors and rowers. In the 1960s and early 1970s, a succession of yachtsmen and women captured the public's imagination with their exploits. Three of them mention religion or spirituality in their accounts. The first was Sir Francis Chichester who, between September 1966 and May 1967, sailed single-handed around the world in *Gipsy Moth IV* at the age of 65. Describing sailing through the Roaring Forties – a notoriously windy stretch of the southern seas – Chichester, like Slocum, experienced intense feelings of solitude. However, for Chichester, the son of a clergyman, it was not a positive experience but a deeply depressing one. 'I find it hard to describe, even put into words at all,' he writes, 'the spiritual loneliness of this empty quarter of the world.' He contrasted this 'great void' of the southern seas with the North Atlantic which, 'seems to have a spiritual atmosphere as if teeming with the spirits of the men who sailed and died there.'[26]

In contrast, Chay Blyth, who between October 1970 and August 1971 sailed around the world single-handed 'the wrong way round' – that is against westerly winds – had an experience similar to Slocum's. 'Ten months of solitude in some of the loneliest seas of the world strengthened every part of me,' he wrote, 'deepened every perception and gave me a new awareness of that power outside man which we call God.'[27] To Robin Knox-Johnston, who between June 1968 and April 1969 became the first person to sail round the world non-stop, single-handed, such an observation is not surprising. Reflecting on the impact of confronting natural elements on the religious beliefs and superstitions of sailors he commented:

> I have found myself thinking deeply on the matter when out in rough weather in a small boat … However practical you like to think you are, the feeling comes that there is more to it than just natural laws, and if you have been brought up in a society that bases its philosophy on the existence of a Superior Being, you come to consider that this Being is responsible, and to accept that he exists.[28]

Roz Savage, the only woman to have rowed single-handed across the Atlantic, Indian, and Pacific oceans, experienced something akin to the oceanic feeling and Joshua Slocum's 'solitude supreme'. While sleeping on deck 'alone in the vast darkness of the [Pacific] ocean', she writes, she found herself 'suddenly marvelling at the strangeness and splendour' of her life, and while looking up at the Milky Way, sensing 'my utter insignificance, and at the same time my complete interconnection with everything' which led to 'a profound sense of joy – which lasted until the clouds blotted out the stars, a squall blew in, and I beat a hasty retreat to the shelter of the cabin.'[29]

The sea, then, has the capacity to touch us at our deepest level. The psalmist used the image of the depths of water speaking to our spiritual depths: 'Deep calls to deep' (Psalm 42:7). This is particularly the case for the sea given its vastness, grandeur, and immense power. The sea fascinates because of its 'otherness' from what we know and experience on land. It can attract, repel, delight, frighten, calm, or heighten anxiety. It can induce feelings of melancholy or delight. The sea's moods are as varied and fluid as water itself. If we wish, we can project onto the sea the full range of human temperament, and the sea has the power to reflect them back. It is, as Conrad suggests, a mirror, not only of the blue sky but of the psyche and soul. Perhaps, as we will now consider, the sea can speak to us of things beyond our comprehension.

1   Catherine Phillips (ed.), *Gerard Manley Hopkins* (Oxford: Oxford University Press, 1986), p. 291.
2   McGilchrist, *The Master*, p. 380.
3   Carl G. Jung, *Memories, Dreams, Reflections* (London: Collins and Routledge and Kegan Paul, 1963), p. 22.
4   Carl G. Jung (eds. Sir H. Read, M Fordham and G. Adler), *The Collected Works*, vols. 1-20 (London: Routledge, 2014), p. 6243, para. 241.
5   Carl G. Jung (trans. Stanley Dell), *The Integration of the Personality* (London: Kegan Paul, Trench, Trubner and Co., 1940), p. 103.
6   Roger Deakin, *Waterlogged: A Swimmer's Journey through Britain* (London: Vintage, 2000), p. 3.
7   Quoted in Elaine Morgan, *The Aquatic Ape: A Theory of Human Evolution* (London: Souvenir Press, 1982), p. 142.
8   Ibid., p. 141.
9   David Hay, *Religious Experience Today: Studying the Facts* (London: Mowbray, 1990), p. 17.
10 Religious Experience Research Centre, University of Wales, Trinity St David. Database account number 912.
11 Thor Heyerdahl, *In the Footsteps of Adam: A Memoir of an Extraordinary Life* (London: Abacus Books, 2001), p. 195.
12 John Steinbeck, *The Log from the Sea of Cortez* (London: Penguin, 1995), p. 178.
13 Religious Experience Database 1346.
14 William James, *The Varieties of Religious Experience* (London: Penguin, 1982), p. 288.
15 Ibid., p. 395.
16 Sigmund Freud, *Civilization and Its Discontents*, in James Strachey and Anna Freud (eds.), *The Standard Edition of the Complete Psychological Works of Sigmund Freud*, Vol. 21 (London: Hogarth Press, 1961), p. 72.
17 Helen M. Rozwadowski, *Fathoming the Ocean: The Discovery and Exploration of the Deep Sea* (Cambridge, MA: Belknap Press, 2005), p. 5.
18 Rudolf Otto, *The Idea of the Holy* (Oxford: Oxford University Press, 1958), pp. 12-13.
19 Ibid., p. 182.
20 E.B. White, 'The Sea and the Wind that Blows', in Jonathan Raban (ed.), *The Oxford Book of the Sea* (Oxford: Oxford University Press, 1993), p. 497.
21 Conrad, *Mirror of the Sea*, p. 7.

22 Ann Spencer, *Alone at Sea: The Adventures of Joshua Slocum* (Buffalo, NY: Firefly Books, 1999), p. 148.

23 Joshua Slocum, *Sailing Alone Around the World* (New York: The Century Co., 1901), p. 256.

24 Ibid., p. 133.

25 Spencer, *Alone at Sea*, p. 149.

26 Francis Chichester, *Gipsy Moth Circles the World* (London: Hodder and Stoughton, 1967), p. 73.

27 Chay Blyth, *The Impossible Voyage* (London: Hodder and Stoughton, 1971), p. 214.

28 Robin Knox-Johnston, *A World of My Own: The Single-Handed, Non-Stop Circumnavigation of the World in* Suhaili, (London: Cassell, 1969), pp. 172-3.

29 Roz Savage, *Stop Drifting, Start Rowing: One Woman's Search for Happiness and Meaning Alone on the Pacific* (London: Hay House, 2013), p.131.

10

The Sacramental Sea

If then a man wishes to know the deepest ocean of
divine understanding, let him first if he is able scan
that visible sea.

Columbanus

In 1375, St Catherine of Siena travelled to Pisa on a peace mission. Known for her political astuteness, Catherine's objective was to prevent war by persuading the leaders of the city states of Pisa and nearby Lucca not to join an anti-papal league. It was on this journey, which involved sailing to the island of Gorgona, that Catherine first saw the sea. Anyone encountering the blue, crystalline waters of the Tuscan Archipelago for the first time is likely to be struck with a sense of awe and wonder. To Catherine, who was then in her late twenties, the effect was profound. As she wrote to her friend, Fr Bartolomeo Dominici, 'I ask you to enter a peaceful sea, by that burning charity, a deep sea. This have I just found out – not that the sea is new, but it is new to me, in my soul's sensing it – in the words "God is love."'[1] For the rest of her life, Catherine associated the sea with God who was, for her, the 'peaceful sea' and the 'sea profound'. Looking into the sea could evoke in Catherine intense religious feelings:

> It is a mirror, reflecting what you, eternal Trinity, let me know because, as I look into this mirror, holding it with the hand of love, it makes me see me, your creature, in you, and you in me by the union that you made of your divinity with our humanity.[2]

This book has explored the spiritual or religious dimension of our relationship with the sea. What will be apparent by now is that over the centuries the sea has fired the imagination and provided a rich source of imagery for theologians, religious poets, writers, and musicians. The experience of being at or by the sea can do more than conjure up ideas and images, however. As Catherine's experience shows, engaging with the sea has the potential to connect us with something deep within or beyond ourselves – with God.

Something else that will be apparent is that attitudes towards the sea have changed considerably over time, at least in western societies. The biblical association of the sea with primordial chaos, leading to fear and terror, has been eroded by more positive connotations, due in part to improved sea navigation, greater scientific understanding, and a growing appreciation of the sublime beauty of nature. The sea, then, has been fluid in terms of how we relate to it. What has remained constant over time, however, is the sense of the sea's 'otherness'. This manifests itself in various ways. For instance, throughout history and across cultures the sea has been largely treated socially and politically as 'non-territory'. In general, it is only when access to resources such as fisheries or oilfields is at issue that questions of ownership of the sea come to the fore. Otherwise, the sea has been largely perceived and treated as neutral, common space. From time to time the sea might come under political control (as was the case of the Mediterranean under the Roman Empire) but never outright ownership. It is this Roman concept that lies behind Hugo Grotius' great legal treatise of 1608 *Mare Liberum* (*The Freedom of the Seas*) which underpins modern ocean law. For Grotius, the sea is a 'common good' available to everyone, and because it is effectively limitless it cannot become the property of anyone. Interestingly, there are calls for this same legal principle to be applied to cyberspace.

In a similar vein, the geographer Philip E. Steinberg argues that the sea is 'not a space of society', and that because of its 'otherness', those who go to sea can find it a place where the norms of society on land are suspended or ignored. There can be social freedom to the point of anarchy in life at sea. Captain Nemo's monologue in Jules Verne's 1870 novel *20,000 Leagues Under the Sea* as a classic example of this attitude. In describing his love for the sea and of being a sub-mariner, Nemo, the story's mysterious anti-hero, concludes:

> The sea does not belong to despots. Upon its surface, men can still exercise unjust laws, fight, tear one another to pieces, and be carried away with terrestrial horrors. But at thirty feet below its level, their reign ceases, their influence is quenched, and their power disappears. Ah! sir, live – live in the bosom of the waters! There only is independence! There I recognise no masters! There I am free![3]

The otherness of the sea, then, seems to permit a different way of life to that on land, with a sense of freedom from the normal constraints of daily living. This freedom is expressed powerfully in John Masefield's 'Sea-Fever', one of the most popular, and evocative, poems in the English language:

I must go down to the seas again, to the lonely sea and the sky,
And all I ask is a tall ship and a star to steer her by,
And the wheel's kick and the wind's song and the white sail's shaking,
And a grey mist on the sea's face, and a grey dawn breaking.

I must go down to the seas again, for the call of the running tide
Is a wild call and a clear call that may not be denied;
And all I ask is a windy day with the white clouds flying,
And the flung spray and the blown spume, and the sea-gulls crying.

I must down to the seas again, to the vagrant gypsy life,
To the gull's way and the whale's way where the wind's like a
    whetted knife;
And all I ask is a merry yarn from a laughing fellow-rover
And quiet sleep and a sweet dream when the long trick's over.

Having lost both parents when he was a child, and after a difficult time at school, Masefield joined the Merchant Navy at the age of thirteen. Perhaps for the young Masefield the prospect of this life offered liberation from a traumatic childhood – 'the vagrant gypsy life'. If so, his early experiences at sea did not lead to immediate happiness. On his first voyage he confronted violent weather and bad sea-sickness. So disillusioned was he with the life of a sailor that the following year he jumped ship in New York and lived for months on its streets. Despite these set-backs, Masefield was captivated by the sea and its liberating effect. Turning instead to fulfilling his childhood ambition to become a writer, he found an outlet to express his deepest feelings about the sea.

Another poet to hear the sea's call is Gwyneth Lewis, the first National Poet of Wales. In her book *Two in a Boat: A Marital Rite of Passage* she describes how, in the 1990s, she took up sailing with her husband largely with the purpose of facing her depression. 'Part of a seaman's knowledge', she writes, 'has always been to deal with the internal hazards of fear, panic and carelessness. This, I thought, might help me move farther away from the depression I suffered at home.'[4] The book is a candid reflection on her experiences, which were far from easy. What come across strongly are not only the effects of living with someone at close quarters and the sailor's discipline, but the impact of the sea on the human spirit. Describing an early trip in the Bristol Channel and reaching the point where the channel opens up at Watchet (the small coastal town that helped inspire Coleridge to write *The Rime of the Ancient Mariner*) she writes, 'Our spirits lifted as we looked south-west into a larger sky. We gazed at the open horizon and were knocked breathless by the freedom it offered.'[5]

Like Masefield, there is a sense in Lewis' account of being drawn to the sea because, by its otherness, it offers something very different to life on land and an environment in which to move on from things that constrain or weigh us down. Despite the confines of life on board a boat, both writers discovered liberation in open waters. Away from the rest of humanity, and in a place where movement is much freer, dictated by the natural forces of wind, current, and tide, those at sea experience something far removed and 'other' from life on land. It is a recurring theme for those who have heard the sea's call. As an oceanographer put it succinctly, 'The land is beautiful; the sea is – different.'[6]

A similar sense of liberation can be experienced by being near the sea. This is something explored by the poet W. H. Auden. In 1937 Auden collaborated with the composer Benjamin Britten to produce the screenplay and soundtrack for a film documentary for Southern Railways, *The Way to the Sea*. This was about a more popular call to the sea made possible by train services to the seaside, when the whole gamut of humanity apparently came in search of freedom to 'build sand castles and dream castles'.[7] As the historian of tourism, John Walton, observes, it is at the seaside that 'the pleasure principle is given freer rein'. Whether it is public bodily exposure or eating food with fingers while walking down a street, it is at the seaside that normal social conventions are suspended or upturned.[8]

While some are drawn to the sea for relaxation, others look for a very different experience. Rough seas can draw sightseers, sailors, and surfers – all seeking the thrill of danger. This is something that intrigued John Steinbeck. In another perceptive passage in *The Log from the Sea of Cortez*, while noting with some irony the higher probability of being killed crossing the road than by sailing, Steinbeck wrote:

> the atavistic urge towards danger persists and its satisfaction is called adventure. However your adventurer feels no gratification in crossing Market Street in San Francisco against the traffic. Instead he will go to a good deal of trouble and expense to get himself killed in the South Seas.[9]

While there have always been those with a sense of adventure who have taken to the seas, psychologist and amateur yachtsman Michael Stadler believes thrill-seeking has increased significantly since the late-twentieth century as a reaction against 'a sheltered, predictable and monotonous urban lifestyle' experienced by many. [10] For such thrill-seekers, the ultimate challenge is to confront the forces of nature. Someone who rose to this challenge was Gearóid Ó Donnchadha, an Irish Roman Catholic priest who twice crossed the Atlantic in small boats. 'Experiencing a major Atlantic storm', he wrote, 'is to meet nature gone mad. The visual element is overpowering. What I can best liken it to is being among the Himalayas except that the mountains are moving, not regularly, but criss-crossing one another in tumultuous frenzy'. Such an experience enhances the sense of isolation whereby, according to Ó Donnchadha:

> the harassment and brutalization of one's sense enters into one's very consciousness so as to create a virtual out-of-body experience where one is bereft of all but the experience of the moment. Relatives, friends, familiar land places are no more. They are stripped from your consciousness. There is only you and the forces of nature. You have been stripped of civilization, of culture; you are left with the most primal instinct of survival. [11]

Yet, this intense sense of isolation can also heighten religious feelings; 'there is a well-known phrase "there are no atheists in the trenches"', he wrote. 'There are no atheists in an Atlantic storm either!' [12]

The sea, then, affects us in many and varied ways and can create images that are allegories of the spiritual life. Looking towards the horizon draws us to the unknown that lies beyond. The sea's varying moods resonate with our experiences of peace and turmoil, joy and sorrow, life and death. Eternal, unfathomable, elusive, powerful, mysterious, apparently infinite, life-giving, yet fearful: in its very essence the sea speaks of God.

The spiritual dimension of the sea is something that the Roman Catholic writer Hilaire Belloc, who was an accomplished sailor, explored in his account of sailing round Britain called *The Cruise of the 'Nona'*. Described by the maritime writer Jonathan Raban as 'the weirdest imaginable blend of *Mein Kampf* and *Yachting Monthly*' (Belloc's disturbing admiration for Mussolini and fascism is evident), *The Cruise of the 'Nona'* is also a kind of catechism. Belloc makes no reference to experiences like those in the

Religious Experience Database. In heavy seas off Bardsey Island, when he faced the prospect of drowning, he recalled: 'I discovered myself to be for the first time in my life entirely indifferent to my fate. It was a very odd sensation indeed.' Describing the experience he wrote,'[it] was about as much like courage as lying in a hammock is like a hundred yards race. It had no relation to courage, nor, oddly enough, had it any relation to religion, or to a right depreciation of this detestable little world which can be so beautiful when it likes.'[13] Nevertheless, the sea did have a profound effect on Belloc as a person of faith. The sea, he wrote, 'presents, upon the greatest scale we mortals can bear, those not mortal powers which brought us into being. It is not only the symbol or the mirror, but especially it is the messenger of the Divine.' From this Belloc concludes that the sea 'is the common sacrament of this world.'[14]

Over the centuries, a number of influential thinkers and writers have emphasised the sacramental dimension of creation: its ability, in the words of Michael Mayne, 'to mirror the Divine'.[15] Among them, the medieval Scottish theologian John Duns Scotus regarded the material world as a sacramental symbol of God. For his near contemporary, the German mystic Meister Eckhart (who faced accusations of heresy), divinity was inseparable from nature. Similarly, the faith of the visionary nun and natural scientist Hildegard of Bingen involved a powerful interaction between theology and nature. Much later, as we have already seen, the priest and poet Gerard Manley Hopkins called the mystical or sacramental quality of nature 'inscape'.

It was Belloc, however, who appreciated more than most the breadth and depth of the sea's sacramental nature. He understood that it could create vivid images to fire the imagination as well as clear the mind to contemplate ultimate mysteries; that at one moment the sea can seem a bountiful source of life, and at another a vast, barren wilderness. He understood, too, that the sea's capricious nature captures precisely the human condition, with its varying moods – and the questions these can throw up about the meaning of life and the nature of God. Such questioning highlights a distinctive aspect of the sea's sacramental nature: the problem of theodicy. On the one hand, the sea is vital to our existence: its place in the hydrologic cycle ensures we are supplied with life-giving water, it is an abundant source of food and, increasingly, a source of energy. It is something that gives pleasure, and is life-enhancing. And yet, at the same time it is dangerous and deadly. Its capricious nature speaks of God as the giver and taker of life, who also permits suffering. There is nothing sentimental about the sea, its dangers are too well known.

What also makes the sea's sacramental nature so profound is that is resonates with the two contrasting approaches to theology and spirituality: the 'kataphatic' and 'apophatic'. The kataphatic approach to religion emphasises what is known and experienced and can be put into words, often by the use of metaphor. It is sometimes described as 'positive' theology or spirituality, and is the dominant approach in Christianity. It is understandable that a religion grounded in the life and teaching of one person, Jesus Christ, should have this emphasis. For Christians, Jesus Christ is both human and divine, and this incarnational understanding of his personhood gives a unique insight into the nature of God in a way that makes the divine tangible. For this reason, Jesus Christ has been called 'the absolute and primary symbol of God in the world.'[16]

The role of the sea in the biblical story of salvation is set firmly within the kataphatic tradition. To the kataphatic mind-set, the sea's vastness speaks of the infinite; its permanence speaks of the eternal and of changelessness; its quixotic fluidity speaks of spirit; its life-giving properties speak of a loving and generous Creator, and its power speaks of the Creator's omnipotence. This, as we have seen, has led the sea to be a rich source of metaphor and imagery in literature and hymnody.

In contrast, the apophatic tradition, or *via negativa*, is grounded in an understanding of God being ineffable: ultimately unknowable and mysterious, and therefore indescribable. Within Christianity, the growth of this tradition owes much to the influence of Neo-Platonism, with its grounding in Classical philosophy and emphasis on the mysterious 'otherness' of the divine. To those drawn to the apophatic tradition, the sea's hidden depths speak of the mysterious and unknowable. More important, however, is the sea's remarkable ability to still and empty the mind. This emptying – or *kenosis* – is at the heart of contemplative prayer in the apophatic tradition. Rather than fill the mind with words and images, apophatic prayer seeks to clear the mind and to allow the void to be filled by God.

Within Christianity, the growth of the apophatic tradition owes much to desert spirituality. One of the reasons that the desert fathers sought barren terrain is that starkness removes distractions and so is an aid to contemplative prayer. As we have seen, this is true also for those who have sought 'a desert in the ocean'. As the monk and sailor Peter F. Anson described from personal experience:

> the call of the 'lonely sea and the sky' is but the voice of Eternity, for the sea drowns out humanity and time – it has no sympathy with either;

for it belongs to Eternity, and it sings its monotonous song of Eternity for ever and ever. Nowhere better than on the sea can one learn what is meant by the 'Loneliness of God'.[17]

By speaking with equal weight to both the kataphatic and apophatic traditions, the sea plays an important role in theology. As Belden C. Lane puts it, there is a 'dialectical tension' between the kataphatic and apophatic traditions, which ultimately need each other.[18] Within Judaism and Christianity there is a profound sense that God is both revealed and hidden, reflecting the experience of many over the centuries of God as mysterious and unknowable, and yet at times seemingly close and familiar. People who have had profound religious experiences of the type analysed by James and Hardy can also experience years of spiritual barrenness.

A number of influential theologians who have wrestled with the tension between apophatic and kataphatic spiritual experiences have been drawn to panentheistic theology. While pantheists regards the divine as being present in all things, pan*en*theists understand God as being both *in* and *beyond* creation. The term panentheism is attributed to the German philosopher Karl Krause, writing in the early nineteenth century, and is particularly associated in the early twentieth century with the theologian William Inge, perhaps best known as a successor to John Donne as Dean of St Paul's. The origins of panentheism are, however, much older. In some respects, panentheism is a development of Thomas Aquinas' understanding of God as 'the ground of being', who not only creates but continues to be involved with creation, sustaining its very existence by grace.

Such an understanding of creation is potentially highly sacramental. If God is regarded as being in some sense within all that is created, then it follows that creation may well in some way reveal something of God. The idea that creation is potentially infinitely sacramental is associated with the twentieth-century Jesuit theologian, Karl Rahner. Rahner regarded Christ as the 'primordial sacrament', who most fully communicates God's self to the world; but he also argued that *everything* has the potential to communicate *something* of God. Drawing on Rahner's work, the contemporary theologian Hans Gustafson has coined the term 'pansacramental' to emphasise the potential of everything created to be a sacrament.[19] Two of Gustafson's insights are particularly relevant to what has been explored in this book. First, he makes clear that some things are more sacramental, or 'God-like', than others. The conclusion of this book is that the sea is highly sacramental: not only, as we have seen, is the sea a potent and multifaceted symbol of God, but it is also associated with religious experience. Sacramentally, the sea connects the transcendent and immanent understanding and experience of God.

This leads to Gustafson's second important insight, the 'sacramental principle' that a sacrament is only a sacrament if we are attuned to seeing the world around us in a sacramental way. Earlier, we discussed the question posed by Richard Dawkins in *The God Delusion*, of why an intense fascination with nature led his former school chaplain towards God and Dawkins himself in the other direction. Another contemporary theologian to have addressed such a question is Alister McGrath. In his critique of natural theology, McGrath points out that what is of primary importance is our disposition towards the natural world. If we are predisposed to see the world through the lens of faith, it will communicate to us differently from how it would if we see it otherwise. Intriguingly, what has been argued throughout this book is that at different times and in different contexts, the sea has been understood theologically in very different ways. From the perspective of an ancient Jewish thought-world, the sea was regarded as the remnant of primordial chaos – a view that persisted into the Middle Ages, as expressed in T-maps such as the *Mappa Mundi*. In contrast to this 'anti-sacramental' view of the sea, it has also been a powerful symbol of God, particularly through the influence of Neo-Platonism. As we have seen, the process of becoming attuned to the sacramental nature of the sea has been long and complicated.

The tensions between the kataphatic and apophatic, of regarding God as imminent and transcendent, and of being attuned – or not – to perceiving the world sacramentally resonates strongly with Iain McGilchrist's understanding of the way the brain uses its left and right hemispheres to make sense of the world. Just as the kataphatic and apophatic need each other, so do the left and right hemispheres of the brain. Just as McGilchrist regards the Enlightenment as displaying left-hemisphere dominance, so too does he see the same phenomenon in the Reformation, with its

> shift away from the capacity to understand metaphor, incarnation, the realm that bridges this world and the next, matter and spirit, towards a literalistic way of thinking – a move away from imagination, now seen as treacherous, and towards rationalism.[20]

In this respect, the emergence of Anglo-Catholicism in the nineteenth century can be seen in similar terms to the rise of Romanticism: while the latter sought to rebalance the influence of Enlightenment thinking, so, too, was the former a reaction against the rise of Protestantism.

A person who embodied the tension between the kataphatic and apophatic traditions was the Trappist monk, social activist, and spiritual writer, Thomas Merton. In 1968, Merton decided to leave the Abbey of Our Lady of Gethsemani in Kentucky where he had lived for 27 years; he now wanted to seek solitude in a new location. Merton considered moving to Alaska and the New Mexican desert, but, after spending four days alone in a small farmhouse on the wild and remote 'lost coast' of north California, he felt he had found the ideal location for his hermitage. As Merton recorded in his journal:

> Northern California was unforgettable. I want very much to go back. Especially to Bear Harbor, the isolated cove on the Pacific shore … the barrier, the reef, the eucalyptus trees, the steep slopes crowned by fir, the cove full of drift-redwood logs, black sand, black stones, and restless sea – the whole show, those deserted pyramids, the hollow full of wild iris, the steep road overhanging the sea, Needle Rock.[21]

Merton refers to the sea as 'restless'. Merton himself was restless, and perhaps his choice of word was significant. Merton's restlessness was at least partly due to the dialectic tension of being drawn to the apophatic, as a contemplative, and also the kataphatic, as the incarnational theology of Jesus Christ had led him to be a social activist. Living with this tension, Merton appears never to have felt truly at home in the world, and perhaps that led him to look to relocate from Gethsemani. After returning to Kentucky from California he wrote in his journal:

> Lonely for the Pacific and the Redwoods. A sense that somehow when I was there I was unutterably happy – and maybe I was. Certainly, every minute I was there, especially by the sea, I felt I was at home – as if I had come a very long way to where I really belonged.[22]

Elsewhere in his journal Merton expands on what he meant by 'home', which he expresses in highly apophatic terms: 'The country which is nowhere is the real home; only it seems that the Pacific Shore at Needle Rock is more nowhere than this, and Bear Harbor is more nowhere still.'[23]

Whether or not Merton had truly found his spiritual as well as physical home on the Pacific coast, no one knows. Just a few weeks later, Merton was found dead in a hotel room in Bangkok, apparently electrocuted by a fan with faulty wiring.

On 11 December 1962, almost six years to the day before his death, Merton wrote the following in his journal: 'Very cold. Some snow. Bright, silent afternoon. / I have been shocked at a notice of a new book, by Rachel

Carson'.[24] Carson was an American marine biologist, whose trilogy *Under the Sea-Wind, The Sea Around Us,* and *The Edge of the Sea* had gained her international recognition as a naturalist and science writer. The book that came to Merton's attention was *Silent Spring.* Published earlier that year, this was Carson's response to the misuse of pesticides and their effect on the environment, in which she called for a fundamental change in our attitude towards the natural world. *Silent Spring* is now widely regarded as key to the development of the environmental movement. For Merton, the book was key to sparking his thinking on ecology.

After reading *Silent Spring,* Merton wrote to Carson. In a letter dated 12 January 1963, Merton expressed his appreciation for the book, and then offered his own perspective on the fundamental issue it raised. 'What I say now is a religious, not a scientific statement', he wrote:

> That is to say, man is at once part of nature and he transcends it. In maintaining this delicate balance, he must make use of nature wisely, and understand his position, ultimately relating both himself and visible nature to the invisible – in my terms, to the Creator, in any case, to the source and exemplar of all being and all life.
>
> But man has lost his 'sight' and is blundering around aimlessly in the midst of the wonderful works of God. It is in thinking that he sees, in gaining power and technical know-how, that he has lost his wisdom and his cosmic perspective.[25]

Both Carson, from a morally aware scientific perspective, and Merton, from a politically engaged theological perspective, shared a common concern for how humanity was exploiting the natural world. Merton was clearly attuned to experiencing the world sacramentally. As he had written in an earlier journal entry:

> The Lord God is present where the new day shines in the moisture on the young grasses. The Lord God is present where the small wildflowers are known to Him alone. The Lord God passes suddenly, in the wind, at the moment when night ebbs into the ground.[26]

In his writings, Merton expresses something of what Robert Faricy described as 'two possible models' for a Christian attitude towards nature: that of the 'responsible service' of making use of the natural world for human benefit in a sustainable way, as associated with the Benedictine monastic tradition, and that of 'praise and contemplation' of God through a deep gratitude for what God has created, which is central to the Franciscan tradition.[27] As a Cistercian monk, Merton lived under the rule of St Benedict, and so was steeped in the Benedictine tradition. However, before joining the Cistercians Merton had thought seriously about becoming a Franciscan, such had been the attraction of St Francis of Assisi who, as Daniel Horan points out, continued to be an import influence on Merton.[28] The Franciscan attitude towards nature is expressed beautifully in St Francis's 'Canticle of the Sun':

> ... Be praised, my Lord, through all your creatures,
> especially through my lord Brother Sun,
> who brings the day; and you give light through him.
> And he is beautiful and radiant in all his splendour!
> Of you, Most High, he bears the likeness ...

Neither Merton nor Carson, who died in 1964, were aware of the human culpability for climate change and its impact on sea levels and the marine environment. Neither were they aware of the emerging issue of marine pollution and its effects on the food chain of marine creatures and humans. These deeply concerning issues have come to our attention much later. What both Carson and Merton were acutely aware of, however, were the attitudes and behaviour that could lead to such problems arising in the first place. In this respect, what they were arguing is perhaps even more pertinent today than it was half a century ago. Both Carson and Merton shared a concern about the Anthropocene (although they did not use this term), when the ecological impact of human activity is all too apparent. In the Anthropocene, cultivating a sacramental understanding of the natural world has become a pressing theological issue. As Merton pointed out in his letter to Carson, simply relying on human ingenuity to find technological fixes to environmental problems created by humans in pursuit of 'progress' is fundamentally flawed, as 'it seems that our remedies are instinctively those which aggravate the sickness: *the remedies are expressions of the sickness itself*.'[29]

As I hope this book has demonstrated, engaging with the natural world – in this case the sea – as an expression of faith affects our perspectives and attitudes. Looking back though history, the sea has been regarded theologically as, amongst other things, a remnant of primordial chaos, a place of spiritual testing, a tool for evangelisation, and, sacramentally, as a multifarious symbol of God. The remedy to the malaise that concerned Merton and Carson, and that should concern us now, is to cultivate an appreciation for the natural world that fundamentally changes our attitude towards it. What Merton and Carson argued for from their different perspectives was a more respectful and less exploitative attitude towards nature. Such an attitude should flow naturally from a sacramental understanding of the world around us. If we understand that God is in some sense behind and within the created order, then it should follow that we should treat creation with reverence. History proves otherwise, of course, which is why Merton also raised the theological issue of humanity's 'fall' in his letter, and the concept of 'original sin', which he saw in terms of a form of human self-destructiveness.

At the outset of this book we saw that the biblical story of salvation – of divine action to rescue humanity from its 'fallen', sinful state – involves the sea, through the story of the Flood and its various echoes later on. No wonder, then, that people down the ages have interpreted floods and tsunamis as warnings of God's displeasure. Whether or not we share the theological outlook that God intervenes in the world in such a destructive way, it is hard not to draw parallels between the Flood and rising sea levels today. Climate change does occur naturally, and so seas will rise and fall naturally, but the overwhelming scientific evidence for what is currently happening shows that it is largely, if not fully, due to human behaviour. In this sense, it is both a violation of what God has created and an act of self-destruction, as humanity rues the consequences: an echo of the biblical story of Noah, the *Epic of Gilgamesh*, and other ancient stories about floods.

The voyage we set out on at the beginning of this book is now coming to an end, and it is nearly time to disembark. We have travelled on currachs, galleys, steamships, and yachts that have taken us to many places over many years, encountering an extraordinary range of people along the way, whose ideas and experiences speak of the power of the sea to shape lives and mind-sets. Perhaps, as others who undertake long voyages remark, it has opened us to new experiences and ideas, and provided a new perspective on the world around us. If this includes regarding the sea as in some sense sacramental in Dillistone's terms of holding 'more of value or significance within it than at first meets the eye', and in consequence treating it with the reverence and respect that in their different ways Merton and Carson called for, then our spiritual voyage through Christian history will have served its purpose.

1   Giuliana Cavallini, *Catherine of Siena* (London and New York: Continuum, 2005), p. 30.
2   Ibid., pp. 31-32.

3   Jules Verne, *Twenty Thousand Leagues Under the Sea* (Ware: Wordsworth Classics, 1992), pp. 43-44.
4   Gwyneth Lewis, *Two in a Boat: A Marital Rite of Passage* (London: Harper Perennial, 2006), p. 16.
5   Ibid., p. 8.
6   P. Groen, *The Waters of the Sea* (London: D. Van Nostrand, 1967), p. x.
7   Donald Mitchell, *Britten and Auden in the Thirties: The Year 1936* (London: Faber and Faber, 1981), pp. 90 – 2.
8   John K. Walton, *The British Seaside: Holidays and Resorts in the Twentieth Century* (Manchester and New York: Manchester University Press, 2000), pp. 3-4.
9   Steinbeck, *Sea of Cortez*, p. 6.
10 Michael Stadler, *Psychology of Sailing: The Sea's Effects on Mind and Body* (London: Adlard Coles, 1987), pp. 117-8.
11 Gearóid Ó Donnchadha, *St Brendan of Kerry, the Navigator: His Life and Voyages* (Dublin: Open Air, 2004), pp. 8-9.
12 Ibid., p. 28.
13 Ibid., p. 7.
14 Hilaire Belloc, *The Cruise of the 'Nona'* (London: Century Publishing, 1983), 346-7.
15 Michael Mayne, *This Sunrise of Wonder: Letters for the Journey* (London: Darton, Longman and Todd, 2008), p. 71.
16 Hans Gustafson, *Finding All Things in God: Pansacramentalism and Doing Theology Interreligiously* (Eugene, Or.: Picwick, 2016), p. 104.
17 Peter F. Anson, *The Quest of Solitude* (London: Dent, 1932), pp. 262-3.
18 See Belden C. Lane, *The Solace of Fierce Landscapes: Exploring Desert and Mountain Spirituality* (New York and Oxford: Oxford University Press, 1998), especially chapter 3.
19 Gustafson, *Finding All Things in God*.
20 McGilchrist, *The Master*, p. 382.
21 Thomas Merton (ed. Patrick Hart), *The Other Side of the Mountain; The End of the Journey* (San Francisco: HarperSanFancisco, 1999), p. 117.
22 Ibid., p. 122.
23 Ibid., p. 110.
24 Thomas Merton, *Turning Toward the World: The Pivotal Years* (San Francisco: HarperSanFancisco, 1997), p. 274.
25 Thomas Merton (ed. William H. Shannon and Christine M. Bochen), *Thomas Merton: A Life in Letters: The Essential Collection* (Oxford: Lion, 2009), p. 209.
26 Thomas Merton (ed. Jonathan Montaldo), *Entering the Silence: Becoming a Monk and Writer* (San Francisco: Harper Collins, 1996), p. 474.
27 Robert Faricy, *Wind and Sea Obey Him: Approaches to a Theology of Nature*, (London: SCM Press, 1982), p. ix.
28 Daniel Horan, *The Franciscan Heart of Thomas Merton: A New Look at the Spiritual Inspiration of His Life, Thought, and Writing* (Notre Dame, IN: Ave Maria Press, 2014).
29 Merton, *A Life in Letters*, p. 208.

Bibliography

Books

Joseph Addison, *The Works of the Right Honourable Joseph Addison*, vol. 5 (London: T. Cadell and W. Davies, 1811).

Anon., *God's warning to the people of England by the great overflowing of the waters or floods* (London, 1607).

Peter F. Anson, *The Quest of Solitude* (London: Dent, 1932).

Sarah Arenson, *The Encircled Sea: The Mediterranean Maritime Civilisation*, (London: Constable, 1990).

Isaac Asimov, *In the Beginning* (London: New English Library, 1981).

W.H. Auden, The *Enchafèd Flood, or the Romantic Iconography of the Sea* (London: Faber and Faber, 1951).

St. Augustine (trans. Ludwig Schopp), *The Happy Life* (London: B. Herder Book Co., 1939).

Gaston Bachelard, *Water and Dreams: An Essay on the Imagination of Matter* (Dallas: The Pegasus Foundation, 1983).

Margaret Barker, *Temple Theology: An Introduction* (London: SPCK, 2004).

W.R.J. Barron and Glyn S. Burgess (eds.), *The Voyage of St Brendan* (Exeter University Press, 2002).

The Ecclesiastical History of the English Nation by the Venerable Bede (London: J.M. Dent, 1910).

Hilaire Belloc, *The Cruise of the "Nona"* (London: Century Publishing, 1983).

Chay Blyth, *The Impossible Voyage* (London: Hodder and Stoughton, 1971).

Philotheus Boehner and Zachary Hayes (eds.) *Works of St Bonaventure*, vol. 2, *Itinerarium Mentis in Deum* (New York: Franciscan Institute Publications, 2002).

Janet and Colin Bord, *Sacred Waters: Holy Wells and Water Lore in Britain and Ireland* (Paladin, 1986).

Robert Boyle, *The Excellency of Theology Compar'd with Natural Philosophy* (London, 1674).

E.G. Bowen, *Saints, Seaways and Settlements* (Cardiff, 1977).

William Bradford, *History of Plymouth Plantation* (New York: Effingham, Maynard and Co., 1890).

Ian Bradley, *Water: A Spiritual History* (London: Bloomsbury, 2012).

Dan Brayton, *Shakespeare's Ocean: An Ecocritical Exploration* (University of Virginia Press, 2012).

Jerry Brotton, *A History of the World in Twelve Maps* (London: Penguin, 2012).

David Brown, *God and Enchantment of Place: Reclaiming Human Experience* (Oxford: Oxford University Press, 2004).

Walter Brueggemann, *The Message of the Psalms: A Theological Commentary* (Minneapolis: Augsburg, 1984).

William Buckland, *Geology and Mineralogy Considered with Reference to Natural Theology*, vol. 1 (London: William Pickering, 1836).

Frank T. Bullen, *With Christ at Sea: A Personal Record of Religious Experiences on Board Ship for Fifteen Years* (New York: Frederick A. Stokes, 1900).

Edmund Burke (ed, James T. Boulton), *A Philosophical Enquiry into the Origin of our Ideas of the Sublime and Beautiful* (London: Routledge and Kegan Paul, 1958).

Thomas Burnet, *The Theory of the Earth: Containing an Account of the Original of the Earth, and of all the General Changes which it hath already undergone, or is to undergo till the Consummation of All Things* (London, 1697).

Marilyn Butler, *Romantics, Rebels and Reactionaries: English Literature and its Background 1760-1830* (Oxford: Oxford University Press, 1981).

Martin Butlin and Evelyn Joll, *The Paintings of J.M.W. Turner*, revised edn, vol. 1 (New Haven and London: Yale University Press, 1984).

Rachel L. Carson, *The Sea Around Us* (New York: Oxford university Press, 1951).

L. Casson, *Ships and Seamanship in the Ancient World* (Princeton, 1986).

Giuliana Cavallini, *Catherine of Siena* (London and New York: Continuum, 2005).

Francis Chichester, *Gipsy Moth Circles the World* (London: Hodder and Stoughton, 1967).

Nora Chadwick, *The Celts* (London: Penguin, 1997).

Paul H. Chapman, *The Man who Led Columbus to America* (Atlanta, G.A.: Judson Press, 1973).

St John Chrysostom (trans. R.C. Hill), *Eight Sermons on the Book of Genesis* (Boston, MA: Holy Cross Orthodox Press, 2004).

A Clergyman of the Church of England (ed.), *Hymns for the Sea* (London: J and C Mozley, 1865).

Samuel Taylor Coleridge, *The Statesman's Manual; or the Bible the Best Guide to Political Skill and Foresight* (London: Gale and Fenner, 1816).

Christopher Columbus (ed. Roberto Rusconi, tr. Blair Sullivan), *The Book of Prophecies edited by Christopher Columbus* (Berkeley and London: University of California Press, 1997).

Common Worship: Services and Prayers for the Church of England (London: Church House Publishing, 2000).

Joseph Conrad, *The Mirror of the Sea* (New York: Doubleday, Page & Co., 1924).

— *The Nigger of the Narcissus* (New York: Doubleday, 1914).

Alain Corbin (trans. Jocelyn Phillips), *The Lure of the Sea: Discovery of the Seaside in the Western World, 1750-1840* (Penguin, 1995).

Barry Cunliffe, *Facing the Ocean: The Atlantic and Its Peoples, 8000BC to AD 1500* (Oxford University Press, 2004).

— *Europe Between the Oceans: 9000BC to AD1000* (Yale University Press, 2008).

— *On the Ocean: The Mediterranean and the Atlantic from Prehistory to AD 1500* (Oxford: Oxford University Press, 2017).

Nicholas of Cusa (trans. Jasper Hopkins), *Complete Philosophical and Theological Works of Nicholas of Cusa*, vol. 3 (Minneapolis: Arthur J Banning Press, 2001).

Jean Daniélou (trans. W. Mitchell), *Origen* (Eugene: Wipf and Stock, 1955).

Richard Dawkins, *The God Delusion* (London: Transworld, 2006).

John Day, *God's Conflict with the Dragon and the Sea* (Cambridge University Press, 1985).

Roger Deakin, *Waterlog: A Swimmer's Journey Through Britain* (London: Vintage, 2000).

I.C.B. Dear and Peter Kemp (eds.), *Oxford Companion to Ships and the Sea*, 2nd edition (Oxford University Press, 2006).

Carol Delaney, *Columbus and the Quest for Jerusalem*, (London: Duckworth Overlook, 2013).

F.W. Dillistone, *Christianity and Symbolism* (London: Collins, 1955).

Richard Ellis, *Monsters of the Sea: The History, Natural History, and Mythology of the Ocean's Most Fantastic Creatures* (New York: Alfred A. Knopf, 1995).

Brian Fagan, *Fish of Friday: Feasting, Fasting and the Discovery of the New World* (New York: Basic Books, 2006).

A.F. Falconer, *Shakespeare and the Sea* (1964).

Robert L. Faricy, *Wind and Sea Obey Him: Approaches to a Theology of Nature* (London: SCM, 1982).

Ludwig Feuerbach (trans. George Eliot), *The Essence of Christianity* (New York, Cosimo, 2008).

Andrew Gant, *O sing Unto the Lord: A History of English Church Music* (London: Profile Press, 2015).

Henry James Garland, *Henry Francis Lyte and the Story of 'Abide with Me'* (Manchester: Torch publishing, n.d.).

Edmund Gosse *Father and Son: A Study of Two Temperaments* (London: William Heinemann, 1907).

P. Groen, *The Waters of the Sea* (London: D. Van Nostrand, 1967).

Hugo Grotius (trans. Ralph Van Deman Magoffin), *The Freedom of the Seas* (CreateSpace, 2018).

Malcolm Guite, *Faith, Hope and Poetry: Theology and the Poetic Imagination* (Farnham: Ashgate, 2010).

— *Mariner: A Voyage with Samuel Taylor Coleridge* (London: Hodder & Stoughton, 2017).

Herman Gunkel (trans. K. William Whitney), *Creation and Chaos in the Primeval Era and the Eschaton: A Religio-Historical Study of Genesis 1 and Revelation 12* (Cambridge: Eerdmans, 2006).

Hans Gustafson, *Finding All Things in God: Pansacramentalism and Doing Theology Interreligiously* (Eugene, Or.: Pickwick Publications, 2016).

Winston Halapua, *Waves of God's Embrace: Sacred Perspectives from the Ocean* (Norwich: Canterbury Press, 2008).

Edmond Halley, *Some Considerations about the Cause of the Universal Deluge, laid before the Royal Society on the 12th of Dec. 1694.*

Richard Hamblyn, *Tsunami* (London: Reaktion Books, 2014).

James Hamilton-Paterson, *Seven Tenths: The Sea and its Thresholds* (London: Faber and Faber, 2007).

David Bentley Hart, *The Doors of the Sea: Where Was God in the Tsunami?* (Grand Rapids, MI: Eerdmans, 2005).

David Hay, *Religious Experience Today: Studying the Facts* (London: Mowbray, 1990).

— *Something There: The Biology of the Human Spirit* (London: Darton, Longman and Todd, 2006).

— *God's Biologist: A Life of Alister Hardy* (London: Darton, Longman and Todd, 2011).

Thor Heyerdahl (trans. Ingrid Christophersen), *In the Footsteps of Adam: A Memoir of an Extraordinary life* (London: Abacus, 2001).

Robert Hooke, *Micrographia: or Some Physiological Descriptions of Minute Bodies made by Magnifying Glasses with Observations and Inquiries Thereupon* (London, 1665).

Daniel Horan, *The Franciscan Heart of Thomas Merton: A New Look at the Spiritual Inspiration of His Life, Thought, and Writing* (Notre Dame, IN: Ave Maria Press, 2014).

Thomas Hunter, *A Historical Account of Earthquakes, Extracted from the most Authentick Historians* (Liverpool, 1756).

John Inge, *A Christian Theology of Place* (Ashgate, 2003).

William James, *The Varieties of Religious Experience* (London: Penguin, 1982).

Carl G. Jung, *The Integration of the Personality* (London: Kegan Paul, 1940).

— *Memories, Dreams, Reflections* (London: Collins and Routledge and Kegan Paul, 1963).

— (eds. Sir H. Read, M Fordham and G. Adler), *The Collected Works*, vols. 1-20 (London: Routledge, 2014).

Djelal Kadir, *Columbus and the ends of the Earth: Europe's prophetic rhetoric as conquering ideology* (Berkeley: University of California Press, 1992).

William Knight (ed.), *Journals of Dorothy Wordsworth*, vol. 1 (London and New York: Macmillan, 1897).

Robin Knox-Johnston, *A World of My Own: The Single-Handed, Non-Stop Circumnavigation of the World in* Suhaili (London: Cassell, 1969).

Belden C. Lane, *The Solace of Fierce Landscapes: Exploring Desert and Mountain Spirituality* (New York and Oxford: Oxford University Press, 1998).

Brian Lavery, *The Island Nation: A History of Britain and the Sea* (Conway Maritime Press, 2005).

Lena Lenček and Gideon Bosker, *The Beach: The History of Paradise on Earth* (New York: Viking, 1998).

Gwyneth Lewis, *Two in a Boat: A Marital Rite of Passage* (London: HarperPerennial, 2006).

The Works of John Locke, vol. 3 (London: Awnsham Churchill, 1722).

A.A. Long (ed.), *The Cambridge Companion to Early Greek Philosophy* (Cambridge University Press, 1999).

Andrew Louth, *The Wilderness of God* (London: Darton, Longman and Todd, 1991).

Ernest J. Lovell Jr (ed.), *Medwin's Conversations of Lord Byron* (Princeton NJ: Princeton University Press, 1966).

Mary Low, *Celtic Christianity and Nature: Early Irish and Hebridean Traditions* (Edinburgh University Press, 1996).

Ruth Luckhurst, *A Romantic Landscape: The Poems of the Coleridge Way* (private publication, 2014).

Norman Mable, *Popular Hymns and Their Writers*, 2nd edn (London: Independent Press, 1951).

John Mack, *The Sea: A Cultural History* (London: Reaktion Books, 2011).

Barry McDonald (ed.), *Seeing God Everywhere: Essays on Nature and the Sacred* (World Wisdom, 2003).

Robert Macfarlane, *Mountains of the Mind: A History of Fascination* (London: Granta, 2004).

Iain McGilchrist, *The Master and his Emissary: The Divided Brain and the Making of the Western World* (New Haven CT and London: Yale University Press, 2009).

Alister E McGrath, *The Open Secret: A New Vision for Natural Theology* (Oxford: Blackwell, 2008).

– *Re-imagining Nature: The Promise of a Christian Natural Theology*, (Chichester: Wiley Blackwell, 2017).

Michael Mayne, *This Sunrise of Wonder: Letters for the Journey* (London: Darton, Longman and Todd, 2008).

Steve Mentz, *At the Bottom of Shakespeare's Ocean* (London: Continuum, 2009).

Thomas Merton, *Thoughts in Solitude* (London: Burns and Oates, 1997).

— (ed. William H. Shannon), *Witness to Freedom: Letters in Times of Crisis* (San Diego: Harvest Press, 1995).

— (ed. Jonathan Montaldo), *Entering the Silence: Becoming a Monk and Writer* (San Francisco: Harper Collins, 1996).

— (ed. Victor A. Kramer), *Turning Toward the World: The Pivotal Years* (San Francisco: Harper Collins, 1997).

— (ed. Patrick Hart), *The Other Side of the Mountain: The End of the Journey* (San Francisco: HarperSanFrancisco, 1999).

R.W.H. Miller, *One Firm Anchor: The Church and the Merchant Seafarer, an Introductory History* (Cambridge: Lutterworth Press, 2012).

Donald Mitchell, *Britten and Auden in the Thirties: The Year 1936* (London: Faber and Faber, 1981).

R.J. Mitchell, *The Spring Voyage: The Jerusalem Pilgrimage in 1458* (London: John Murray, 1965).

Steven Mithen, *The Singing Neanderthals: the Origins of Music, Language, Mind and Body* (London: Weidenfeld and Nicholson, 2005).

Geoffrey Moorhouse, *Sun Dancing: A Medieval Vision. Seven Centuries on Skellig Michael* (Dublin: The Collins Press, 2009).

Richard Muir, *Approaches to Landscape* (London: Macmillan, 1999).

Elaine Morgan, *The Aquatic Ape: A Theory of Human Evolution* (London: Souvenir Press, 1982).

Stephen Neill, *A History of Christian Missions*, second edition (London: Penguin, 1986).

John Henry Newman, *Apologia Pro Vita Sua: Being A Reply to a Pamphlet entitled 'What, then, does Dr Newman mean?'* (New York: D.Appleton and Co., 1865).

John Newton, *'Out of the Depths': An Autobiography* (Chicago: Moody Press, no date).

— *The Life of the Rev John Newton, Rector of St Mary Woolnoth, London* (New York: American Tract Society, 1830).

Adam Nicolson, *Seamanship: A Voyage Along the Wild Coasts of the British Isles* (London and New York: HarperCollins, 2004).

Peter Noble and Ros Hogbin, *The Mind of the Sailor* (2001).

Wallace J. Nichols, *Blue Mind: How Water Makes You Happier, More Connected and Better at What You Do* (London: Little, Brown, 2014).

Gearóid Ó Donnchadha, *St Brendan of Kerry, the Navigator: His Life and Voyages* (Dublin: Open Air, 2004).

Rudolf Otto (tr. J.W. Harvey), *The Idea of the Holy* (Oxford: Oxford University Press, 1958).

William Paley, *Natural Theology* (New York: American Tract Society, 1886).

Catherine Phillips (ed.), *Gerard Manley Hopkins* (Oxford: Oxford University Press, 1986).

The Travels of Marco Polo the Venetian (London: J.M. Dent, 1908).

Michael Pye, *The Edge of the World: How the North Sea Made Us Who We Are* (London: Penguin Books, 2015).

Jonathan Raban (ed.), *The Oxford Book of the Sea* (Oxford University Press, 1993).

Gerhard von Rad, *Genesis: A Commentary* (London: SCM Press, 1961).

Hugo Rahner, Greek *Myths and Christian Mystery* (London: Burns and Oates, 1963).

Angelo S. Rappoport, *Superstitions of Sailors* (New York: Dover, 2007).

John Ray, *The Wisdom of God Manifested in the Works of Creation*, First Part (London, 1735).

Chet Raymo, *When God is Gone Everything is Holy: The Making of a Religious Naturalist* (Nore Dame, Ind.: Sorin Books, 2008).

Christina Rees, *Sea Urchin: A Childhood at Sea* (Croton-on-Hudson NY: North River Press, 1990).

The Works of J.J. Rousseau, vol. 9 (Edinburgh: John Donaldson, 1774).

Helen M. Rozwadowski, *Fathoming the Ocean: The Discovery and Exploration of the Deep Sea* (Cambridge MA: Belknap Press, 2005).

Charlotte Runcie, *Salt on Your Tongue* (London: Canongate, 2019).

Roz Savage, *Stop Drifting, Start Rowing: One Woman's Search for Happiness and Meaning Alone on the Pacific*, (London: Hay House, 2013).

Verena Schiller, *A Simplified Life: A Contemporary Hermit's Experience of Solitude and Silence* (Norwich: Canterbury Press, 2010).

David Scott, *Beyond the Drift: New and Selected Poems* (Hexham: Bloodaxe Books, 2015).

John Sephton, *Eirik the Red's Saga* (Liverpool: D. Marples and Co., 1880).

Tim Severin, *The Brendan Voyage* (London: Arrow, 1978).

Sylvie Shaw and Andrew Francis, *Deep Blue: Critical Reflections on Nature, Religion and Water* (London: Equinox, 2008).

Philip Sheldrake, *Living Between Worlds: Place and Journey in Celtic Spirituality* (London: Darton, Longman and Todd, 1995).

— *Spirituality and Theology: Christian Living and the Doctrine of God* (London: Darton, Longman and Todd, 1998).

— *Spaces for the Sacred: Place, Memory and Identity* (London: SCM Press, 2001).

Margaret Silf, *At Sea With God* (London: Darton, Longman and Todd, 2003).

Ronald A. Simkins, *Creator and Creation: Nature in the Worldview of Ancient Israel* (Peabody MA: Hendrickson, 1994).

Joshua Slocum, *Sailing Alone Around the World* (New York: The Century Co., 1901).

James Smith, *The Voyage and Shipwreck of St Paul* (Grand Rapids, MI: Baker Book House, 1978).

Ann Spencer, *Alone at Sea: The Adventures of Joshua Slocum* (Buffalo NY: Firefly Books, 1999).

Meric Srokosz and Rebecca S. Watson, *Blue Planet, Blue God: The Bible and the Sea* (London: SCM Press, 2017).

Michael Stadler, *Psychology of Sailing: The Sea's Effect on Mind and Body* (London: Adlard Coles Ltd, 1987).

John Steinbeck, *The Log from the* Sea of Cortez (London: Penguin, 1995).

Philip E. Steinberg, *The Social Construction of the Ocean* (Cambridge, Cambridge University Press, 2001).

W.R.W. Stephens, *Saint John Chrysostom: His Life and Times*, 2nd edn. (London: John Murray, 1880).

H.S. Thayer (ed.), *Newton's Philosophy of Nature: Selections from His Writings* (New York: Dover, 2005).

Benjamin Thorpe, *Codex Exoniensis: A Collection of Anglo-Saxon Poetry* (London: Society of Antiquaries of London, 1842).

Greg Tobin, *The Wisdom of St Patrick: Inspirations from the Patron Saint of Ireland* (New York: Ballantine Books, 1999).

John F. Travis, *The Rise of the Devon Seaside Resorts 1750-1900* (Exeter: University of Exeter Press, 1993).

Yi-Fu Tuan, *The Hydrologic Cycle and the Wisdom of God* (Toronto, 1968).

Jules Verne, *Twenty Thousand Leagues Under the Sea* (Ware: Wordsworth Classics, 1992).

Voltaire (trans. J. McCabe), *Toleration and Other Essays* (New York and London: G.P. Putnam's sons, 1912).

John K. Walton, *The British Seaside: Holidays and Resorts in the Twentieth Century* (Manchester and New York: Manchester University Press, 2000).

Monica Weis, *The Environmental Vision of Thomas Merton* (Lexington KT: University of Kentucky Press, 2011).

Charles Wesley (ed. J. Telford) *The Journal of the Rev. Charles Wesley. The Early Journal, 1736-1739* (London 1910).

John Wesley, *A Survey of the Wisdom of God in the Creation: or A Compendium of Natural Philosophy*, vol. 2 (New York: Methodist Episcopal Church, 1823).

John Wilkinson, *Egeria's Travels* (Warminster: Aris and Phillips, 1999).

David J. Williams, *Paul's Metaphors: Their Context and Character* (Peabody, Mass.: Hendrickson, 1999).

John Withington, *Flood* (London: Reaktion Books, 2013).

Ellen van Wolde, *Stories of the Beginning: Genesis 1-11 and Other Creation Stories* (London: SCM Press, 1996).

William Wollaston, *The Religion of Nature Delineated* (London, 1725).

Tom Wright, *Paul: A Biography* (London: SPCK, 2018).

Articles

John Anderson, 'The Voyage of Brendan, an Irish Monastic Expedition to Discover the Wonders of God's World', *The American Benedictine Review*, 43:3 (September 1992).

Peter Borsay, 'A Room with a View: Visualising the Seaside, c.1750-1914', *Transactions of the Royal Historical Society* 23 (2013).

Edward A. Bryant and Simon K. Haslett, 'Was the AD1607 Coastal Flooding Event in the Severn Estuary and Bristol Channel (UK) due to a Tsunami?' *Archaeology in the Severn Estuary*, 13 (2002).

— 'The AD 1607 Coastal Flood in the Bristol Channel and Severn Estuary: Historical Records from Devon and Cornwall (UK)', *Archaeology in the Severn Estuary*, 15 (2004).

— 'Catastrophic Wave Erosion, Bristol Channel, United Kingdom: Impact of Tsunami?' *Journal of Geology*, 115(3): (2007) 253-270.

Titus Burckhardt, 'The Symbolism of Water', in Barry McDonald (ed.), *Seeing God Everywhere: Essays on Nature and the Sacred*, (Bloomington, Indiana: World Wisdom, 2003).

Pascal Caillet, 'Authorising Authority: John Donne's Sermon to the Virginia Company (1622)', *Revue de la Société d'Études Anglo-Americaines des XVIIe et XVIIIe siècles*, 66 (2009).

Russell R. Dynes, 'The Dialogue between Voltaire and Rousseau on the Lisbon Earthquake: The Emergence of a Social Science View', *International Journal of Mass Emergencies and Disasters*, 18 (2000).

Eucherius of Lyon, 'In Praise of the Desert. A Letter to Bishop Hilary of Lérins', in Tim Vivian, Kim Vivian and Jeffrey Burton Russell (eds.), *The Lives of the Jura Fathers*, (Kalamazoo: Cistercian Publications, 1999).

Sigmund Freud, 'Civilization and Its Discontents' in James Stratchey and Anna Freud (eds.), *The Standard Edition of the Complete Psychological Works of Sigmund Freud*, volume 21 (London: Hogarth Press, 1961).

Michael Ireland, 'Veleky Bog: How Great is Our God! The story behind how a thunderstorm in Sweden prompted the writing of How Great Thou Art, one of Christianity's greatest and much-loved hymns, ASSIST News Service (Sunday, October 7, 2007); http://www.assistnews.net/Stories/2007/s07100068.htm.

David Jacoby, 'Ports of pilgrimage to the Holy Land, Eleventh-Fourteenth Century: Jaffa, Acre, Alexandria', in *The Holy Portolano: The Sacred Geography of Navigation in the Middle Ages*, (Berlin: De Gruyter, 2014).

Bernard McGinn, 'Ocean and Desert as Symbols of Mystical Absorption in the Christian Tradition', *Journal of Religion*, 74 (1994).

Clair McPherson, 'The Sea a Desert: Early English Spirituality and *The Seafarer*', *American Benedictine Review*, 38 (1987).

Elizabeth Struthers Malbon, 'The Jesus of Mark and the Sea of Galilee', *Journal of Biblical Literature* 103 (1984).

Pauline Moffitt Watts, 'Prophecy and Discovery: On the Spiritual Origins of Christopher Columbus's "Enterprise of the Indies"', *American Historical Review*, 90 (1985).

Jonathan Moo, 'The Sea That is No More: Rev 21:1 and the Function of Sea Imagery in the Apocalypse of John', *Novum Testamentum* 51 (2009).

Edmund Newell, The Sacramental Sea', *Anglican Theological Review*, 100 (2018).

R. Steven Notley, 'The Sea of Galilee: Development of an Early Christian Toponym', *Journal of Biblical Literature* 128 (2009).

Thomas O'Loughlin, 'Living in the Ocean', in Cormac Bourke (ed.), *Studies of the Cult of Saint Columba*, (Dublin: Four Courts Press, 1997).

Marjorie O'Rourke Boyle, 'Cusanus at Sea: The Topicality of Illuminative Discourse', *Journal of Religion*, 71 (1991).

Anthony Parr, 'John Donne, Travel Writer', *Huntingdon Library Quarterly*, 70 (2007).

Robert Rosenblum, 'The Abstract Sublime', *ARTnews*, 59 (February 1961).

E.B. White, 'The Sea and the Wind that Blows', in Jonathan Raban (ed.), *The Oxford Book of the Sea*, (Oxford: Oxford University Press, 1993).

Matthew White, Amanda Smith, Kelly Humphryes, Sabine Pahl, Deborah Snelling and Michael Depledge, 'Blue Space: The importance of water for preference, affect, and restorative ratings of natural and built scenes', *Journal of Environmental Psychology*, 30 (2010).

J. M. Wooding, 'St Brendan's Boat: Dead Hides and the Living Sea in Columban and Related Hagiography', in John Carey, Máire Herbert and Padraig Ó Riain (ed), *Studies in Irish Hagiography. Saints and Scholars* (Dublin: Four Courts Press, 2001).

Websites

ASSIST News Service (Sunday, October 7, 2007); http://www.assistnews.net/Stories/2007/s07100068.htm

Brigham Young University: John Donne Sermons, https://contentdm.lib.byu.edu/digital/collection/JohnDonne

Maps

The British Isles

The Mediterranean

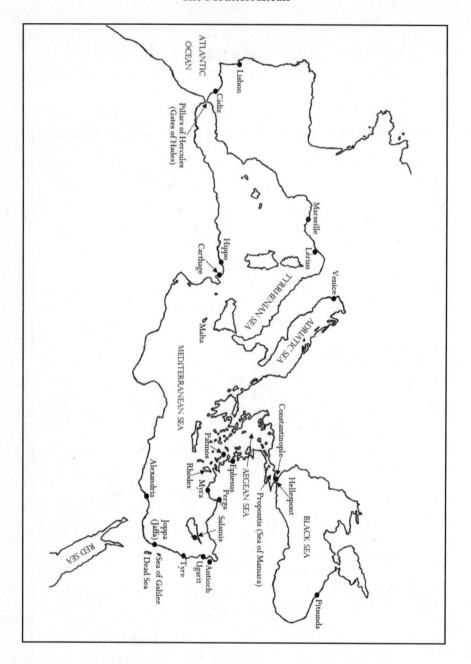

Voyages of Discovery

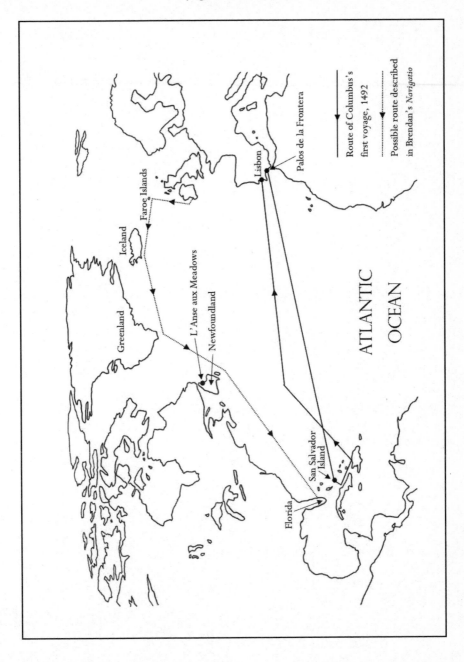

Index of Scriptural References

27 33
27:25 28
27:44 28

1 Corinthians
4:1 34
12:28 34

2 Corinthians
11:25 28

Galatians
2:12 34

Revelation
13 30
15:1 30
15:2 29-30
15:3-4 30
20 30
21:1 30

General Index